CHILD OF THE CROSSFIRE

A True Story

Alcyon

Ruth

Fleck

R

REVIEW AND HERALD® PUBLISHING ASSOCIATION
HAGERSTOWN, MD 21740

The author assumes full responsibility for the accuracy of all facts
and quotations as cited in this book.

This book was
Edited by Penny Estes Wheeler
Designed by Pierce Creative/Matthew Pierce
Cover illustration by Marcus Mashburn
Typeset: 11/15 Palatino

PRINTED IN U.S.A.

03   5 4 3

R&H Cataloging Service
Fleck, Alcyon Ruth, 1921-
    Child of the cross fire: a true story.

    I. Title.

                [B]

ISBN 0-8280-1404-3

Dedication

Several people have especially contributed to the background and effort in writing this story. At the top of the list is my own family—my husband, Ken, and children, Ron, Carolyn, Alicia, and Rick.

They encouraged and supported me in my decision 20 years ago to dedicate my energies and time to homeless and abandoned children. They have continued to free me for that demanding role, and then to write this incredible story of one of our children.

To them I lovingly dedicate this book.

To order additional copies of *Child of the Cross Fire,* by
Alcyon Ruth Fleck, call **1-800-765-6955.**

Visit us at *www.rhpa.org* for more information on
Review and Herald products.

Introduction

*T*his is a true story, written with the prayer that those who read it will be inspired anew to trust in God's unfailing love.

This story is also written to illustrate the truth of the promise in Psalm 68:5, that God is the Father of the fatherless, and these children are the object of His love and concern.

We can have the privilege of being God's hands and feet down here on earth to show His love to abandoned, orphaned, and suffering children. I have learned that there is nothing so effective in healing their trauma and emotional wounds as the love and security of a Christian home and the power of God's love in their lives.

While the facts of this story are true, some of the names of people and places have been changed because of the sensitive issues involved.

God bless you as you read about the little rebel.

ALCYON RUTH FLECK

Prologue

I looked across the table at the young man who had come in response to my request. "I hear you have a story to tell, Salvador," I said. "I have heard about it from others, but I want to hear it from you."

"It's a long story, Mami Fleck. I haven't told it to many people because it is not an easy story to tell. But if you want me to, I will tell it to you."

"Just start at the beginning," I encouraged him. "We have all afternoon."

In the distance we could hear the sounds of children's voices and laughter. We looked through the open door and across the field and saw a group of boys playing soccer. Their happy shouts mingled with the chirps of birds in the nearby trees. A hornet droned outside the screened window. We were at El Bosque, a country campus of homes for orphaned and abandoned children.

But as Salvador began speaking, I was lost to our surroundings. For the next four hours I was transported to another time and place.

Chapter 1

Manuel anxiously waited just outside the bedroom door where his wife, Magdalena, had been struggling for hours with the birth of their baby. Periodically, the old midwife shuffled out to get another cup of the native brew that was supposed to help mothers in labor.

Magdalena's mother had spent the past few days with them, and Manuel was thankful she was there. The grandma took over when it was obvious that the young mother's time had come. She warmed up the beans and tortillas for Manuel and the children and cleaned the kitchen. Then she saw to getting the children into bed. The older boys, Manuel's sons by a former marriage, were off with their uncle at one of the cattle corrals. Because of the distance, they often camped in a cabin there.

Grandma went to check on Magdalena and asked the midwife, "How is she? Do you think it will be much longer?"

"Who knows?" the old lady replied. "Sometimes this happens. We just have to let nature take its course."

When the grandma came out to give Manuel the report, his face was anxious. "Is there nothing anyone can do?"

The young father was remembering that the mother of his older children had died in childbirth. In this remote village there was no hospital and no doctor. Although the village midwives were experienced, they had their limitations. The grandma tried to reassure him. "This happens with some mothers. Remember that Ana's birth was not easy either."

"But it wasn't this long," he insisted.

When the midwife came into the kitchen again, Manuel jumped up from his chair. "How is she doing?" he asked, his voice full of concern.

But the answer was the same. "She is doing as well as can be expected. I'll tell you as soon as there's any change."

This would be their second child. Their first was a girl, named Ana after Magdalena's mother. In the Gomez family, lots of children were considered to be a blessing, and they hoped this would be a boy. Manuel paced the floor, flinching with each cry of pain from his wife's room. Would this never end!

Waiting alone through the long night, the young father had plenty of time for reflection. He thought of the days when they were first married and the pain that her father's attitude had caused Magdalena. Old Don Juan, according to his family tradition, expected her to marry a man who had something to offer her. He knew that this suitor and his family were poor. He considered himself to be an importanat citizen of the community and a land owner. Why couldn't his daughter choose a husband from a good family, and someone closer to her own age?

Manuel was one of eight sons, and he himself had seven sons by his first marriage. After the loss of their mother, he had fallen in love with Magdalena.

Both of his parents had died when their boys were young. As soon as he was old enough he worked by the day for farmers in that area. Since Manuel was the oldest of his seven brothers, he set the pace. He was still a day laborer when he met Magdalena. She was only 15. When her parents realized that she'd fallen in love with a man who, besides being poor, was 10 years her senior they were very unhappy.

"You cannot marry that good-for-nothing," her father declared. "He has nothing to offer you."

While it was the custom in her culture to submit to her father's judgment in finding a husband, Magdalena could not bring herself to forget this man she loved. But no amount of pleading or tears changed her father's mind. Manuel could hardly bring himself to rebel against her father, but the young couple saw no other alternative. They saw each other secretly for a while, and when Don Juan wouldn't give in, they determined to marry without his consent. In his eyes, that was unforgivable, and he refused to let them come home.

The new bride was sad to be separated from her family, but her faith in Manuel was strong. "Don't worry, my dearest," he consoled her. "We'll work hard. Your father will see that I can be trusted to provide for you, and he will change. Just be patient."

Manuel and Magdalena could not be considered a

religious family, although they sometimes attended festivals sponsored by the local parish. Growing up, Magdalena and her family had attended the village church on a regular basis. The rituals were part of her childhood, but as she grew to womanhood, she entertained doubts. Still, she knew there was a God, even though she didn't know how to relate that God to her own life.

When she married Manuel, thoughts of religion were pushed back into a corner of her mind. Maybe someday she would give it more importance, but for now she was too busy.

Manuel had less of a religious background than his wife, but he, too, recognized that there must be a supreme being, although he had no idea what this could have to do with him. He farmed his extensive lands with his seven brothers. The Gomez brothers were becoming known as some of the most successful farmers in that area. Although they did not attend church, Manuel was honest and lived according to the principles of character he had learned as a child. "Remember that you are a Gomez," Manuel's father had taught his children. "You must live up to your name."

Manuel believed that if he was honest, a good neighbor, and provided for his family, that made him a good man. He didn't really need the church. He could handle the problems that came his way without attending Mass, going to confessions, and paying into the church coffers.

Now waiting alone through the agonizing hours of Magdalena's labor, Manuel thought of her father, Don Juan, and how angry he'd been when they married against his will. But he'd been determined to win the old man.

No matter how Don Juan treated him this son-in-law was always respectful. Soon he became aware that Manuel already owned land. They'd built their home on one section and they already owned other adjoining properties. Magdalena's mother grieved over the estrangement with the young family. One day she broached the subject. "You know, Juan, Manuel has just added another large acreage to his farm, and they are living comfortably in their own home. Don't you think it is time that we forget the past?"

The older man sat in his chair near the table, looking at the floor. "Maybe I was wrong. I can't help admiring Manuel. He doesn't even seem to hold a grudge against me; he even comes by to offer his help sometimes."

Encouraged, his wife suggested, "How would it be to invite Maggie and her family to come for a celebration on her birthday? It's only three weeks away."

"That's a good idea," Don Juan agreed. "You know I was only interested in her welfare." The proud old man tried to justify his actions without humbling himself too much. He knew that his wife was never in favor of driving their daughter away.

The birthday party was a huge success, and Magdalena was ecstatic. Manuel was happy too—first of all for his wife's sake, and also because he could now hold up his head with his father-in-law. From then on things began to return to normal. Don Juan, who was a good businessman, soon realized that he could be proud of his son-in-law. Manuel never held the painful years against him, and that fact endeared him more and more to his father-in-law. Not only did he learn to appreciate Manuel for his generous, kind ways, but others in the village with whom he had dealings had the same impression.

From the day they were married, Manuel knew that Magdalena was his most precious possession. He would do anything to take care of her and make her happy. But sitting at his table, his head in his hands, he knew there was nothing he could do to help her now. They lived at least 17 kilometers from the village, but even there only midwives were available for births. Without adequate medical care, it wasn't unusual to hear of the midwives losing a baby, and sometimes a mother. Now, as he sat helplessly listening to her cries, the thought of losing her filled him with terror. In desperation he thought, *If there is a God, does He care about people like us?*

Somehow, despite his ignorance, his heart reached up to this Supreme Being. "If You really exist, God, please help Magdalena." He wondered, *Is this my fault? Maggie always went to church before she married me.*

Hours later he suddenly realized that his wife's cries had ceased. And then came that most beautiful of sounds—the thin cry of a newborn baby. He couldn't wait any longer, but went to the door just as Grandma was coming out. "Is Maggie all right?"

Relief flooded his whole being at the smile on her face. "Yes, Manuel, I think our Maggie will soon be better, and you have a son! We'll let you see them both in just a few minutes."

"Gracias a Dios!" ("Thanks be to God"), he breathed, slumping into a chair. During those long hours Manuel

had realized just how much his family, and especially his young wife, meant to him.

Magdalena was not just any woman. He'd known this from the first time he saw her. Although most men in his culture relegated women to the background, sometimes even into a servile position, Magdalena didn't fit into that mold.

While she didn't interfere in his business, she was interested in everything, and he trusted her judgment enough to seek her opinion many times. In his country, his village, and his family, women knew their place, and most of them accepted the fact that their role was to be a good, obedient wife and to bear and raise a large family with all that it entailed. Magdalena accepted that role, but her and Manuel's relationship was different from that of most of her friends and their husbands.

Now knowing that his wife and baby were safe, Manuel relaxed for the first time and dozed off, his head on his arms on the kitchen table.

He awoke with a start when the door opened. The old midwife was coming, and in her arms she cradled the baby. "Here is your new son, Don Manuel. He is a perfect baby, and a beautiful one, too, don't you think?" His mother-in-law stood by smiling with joy.

He jumped to his feet, reaching out for this new little life—his son. With seven other sons, it was not a new experience, but at that moment, Manuel knew that this, his first son by Magdalena, was very special. His heart filled with love and pride, and yes, gratitude to that God he had appealed to, even though so unknown to him.

"He is beautiful." The father's face simply beamed. "But how is Magdalena?"

"She is fine too, but very tired. You can go in and see her."

Stepping into the room, he asked softly, "Maggie, are you OK?"

"Yes, I think so. Did you see the baby?"

"Yes, Maggie. He's perfect! You have given me a son!"

After the old midwife went home and Grandma had gone to bed, Manuel sat at the kitchen table looking out the window. Dawn was breaking. His ranch lands stretched toward the mountains. The long, worrisome night had left him bone weary, and emotionally exhausted, but a new emotion filled his heart. *I've been through this before, but this time I feel different,* he mused. Without really understanding why, Manuel sensed that this baby was special. Could it be that he was a gift from God? Little did he dream what lay ahead for him.

Chapter (2)

The Gomez household soon settled back into their normal routine, and the new baby, Oscar, was very much a part of it. They lived in the comfortable adobe home on their farm. But instead of being built of adobe bricks, their house, like many others in that mountain area, was framed with wood, making forms that were then filled with a special clay mud. When the mud dried it became very hard, and the thick adobe walls roofed with clay tiles both provided protection from the cold and kept the house cool on hot days.

The main room was large and easily held the long, hand-hewn wooden table where the family gathered for meals. In a corner was a large flat rock conveniently placed on a pedestal. This was where, with a cylindrical stone, Magdalena ground the presoaked corn down to a fine, damp meal. She made tortillas from this meal every morning. Meals were cooked on the woodstove in the corner. It was made of bricks. The smoke escaped through a hole in the wall above the stove. Just outside the door was a stack of firewood. The fire never seemed to go out, and black beans, stew, or soup usually simmered toward the back of the stove.

Every morning the corn was ground for the tortillas. Before the noon meal, one could hear the *slap, slap, slap* of the tortillas being formed and tossed from one hand to the other. Quickly the stack of hot tortillas grew in the towel-covered basket. Modern conveniences were unknown in this typical Mayan home, but the methods used by generations seemed adequate.

Baby Oscar was never far from his mother, either in the basket in the corner, or in the sling—the hand-woven shawl—on her back. The rhythm of her movements as she worked soothed the baby. Magdalena had learned to sing as a young girl, even singing in parts with other children at their parish church. Now she sang as she worked in her home, and little Oscar rested and slept to the comforting sound of his mother's voice.

Mealtimes were busy with Manuel and all the children trooping in to eat. "How's my beautiful little son?" the father would exclaim, picking him up. On these occasions Magdalena would smile to herself and think, *I'm afraid this little boy is going to get spoiled by his father.*

As months flew by, Manuel and Magdalena watched their baby grow into a toddler. Manuel couldn't wait until he could take the little fellow with him out to the fields. As soon as he could walk well enough, he'd scoop him up in his arms and take him along. Soon Oscar learned to know when his father was going out on the farm, and would lift up his little arms and beg to go.

"I'm going to check on the corn crop, Maggie," Manuel said one day, picking up his straw hat. "I'll take

Oscar with me. He has to learn to be a farmer too." The little boy was already walking.

"Don't be gone too long," she warned. "It looks like a rainstorm is coming up."

Oscar had already found his little straw hat and was at the door ready to go. He ran along behind his father. Sometimes when the path got rough Manuel picked him up. As they walked through the rows of corn—higher than Manuel's head—he checked different ears to determine when the field should be harvested. He didn't notice the black clouds coming in from the west. Soon big drops began to fall.

"Oh no!" he cried. "We're going to get soaked." Picking up his son, he placed him on his shoulders and dashed back down the path. He ran for the nearest tree, a large oak, where they could be somewhat sheltered until the storm was past. But they were both thoroughly soaked before reaching home. It was exciting, and more than that it must have been a high adventure. For some reason, that day with his father in the storm stood out as a highlight in the boy's memory.

When they got back home dripping wet Magdalena was worried. "We must get off these wet clothes quickly. We don't want Oscar to get sick!" Soon father and son were dry and warm. Both parents realized that their concern for this little son was different than what they felt for the other children. Although he was healthy, he was somewhat smaller for his age and of a more slender build. All of the Gomez boys felt happy and secure as they grew, but little Oscar was especially embraced—not only with the love and care of his parents, but of the whole family. Early on, he showed a sensitivity that set him apart from the other boys.

As he grew bigger, Oscar went with his father more and more. When going to the farther fields to check on the cattle, Manuel often took him as well as some of the other boys along. Oscar loved those excursions. Sometimes they were gone all day, eating a lunch prepared by Magdalena.

One evening, as they often did, husband and wife sat on the trunk of a fallen oak in their yard, facing the setting sun. "Our boy is growing fast," Manual said proudly. "He can almost keep up with the rest of us, and he loves to get behind those big old steers and yell at them."

Magdalena smiled as she sighed. "Yes, I guess we won't have a baby anymore. He thinks he should do everything his father does."

The next day Manuel and the older boys left to round up the cattle that had been feeding on the farthest slopes of their land. Oscar was left at home with his mother and sister. At first he just looked wistfully after the men, but his mother had a good cure for his disappointment. "I'm going to the river to wash clothes today. Do you want to go along?"

"Oh goody! Can I go?" The gloomy face turned to smiles.

The river was on their own property, and Magdalena led the way to a protected little pool where she did the family washings. It was just the right depth, and the top of a large flat rock—perfect for scrubbing the clothes—stuck out into the water. She carried one basket on her head, and another with her hand. Oscar and his sister, Ana, ran happily along behind her.

Magdalena's favorite wash area was just upstream from a shallow pool where the children could play. The day was warm, and the water not too cold. The children played and splashed with abandon. Soon the soap bubbles from the wash came floating downstream, and they competed with each other to see how many they could catch.

As each garment was washed, Magdalena spread it over nearby bushes to dry in the sun. When she'd finished the last of the heavy men's pants, she grabbed each child and gave them each a good scrubbing. Then she bathed herself. With the clothes draped on nearby bushes to dry, she spread out a blanket and opened a basket of food. The tortillas filled with mashed black beans disappeared fast. Then while the children played, Magdalena rested until the clothes were dry enough to fold into the basket. Wash day was such fun that Oscar forgot all about being left behind by his father.

Magdalena's days were filled with caring for her family. She did her daily tasks in much the same way as her mother, grandmother, and their ancestors had done for centuries. As soon as they were old enough daughters shared in the burdens of the home, and their dreams for the future centered around a good husband, a home, and children. Magdalena had heard the older members of the family tell about their ancestors, and she fully expected that her life would be much the same—a peaceful, predictable life. She could not imagine the storm clouds that lurked on her horizon.

Chapter 3

*T*hree little girls followed after Oscar's birth—Teresa, Margarita, named after Magdalena's sister, and Magdalena, named for her mother and great-grandmother. No longer the baby of the family, Oscar gravitated more and more to his new role as his father's shadow.

"I'm going to check on some new calves tomorrow," Manuel announced at the supper table one evening. "I wonder who wants to go with me."

"Me! Me!" Oscar shouted." Now 5 years old, this youngest son was the one who always wanted to follow his father. The other boys often went, especially when Manuel needed more help. Sometimes he only wanted company. But this time the other brothers were glad that Oscar wanted to go. They had other plans for the day.

Oscar awoke early and pulled on his clothes. He could hear his mother stoking the fire in the kitchen, and he knew that breakfast would soon be ready. The other boys were still in bed.

"Well! What gets you up so early in the morning?" his mother asked with a smile.

"I'm going with Papa to see the calves!" Oscar answered. "Where is he?"

"He's outside. Don't worry; he won't leave you. Breakfast will soon be ready, and you'd better fill up. You'll have a long walk."

Soon the family took their places at the table, and the fried eggs and warmed-up beans began to disappear. There was the hot corn coffee, made from corn that had been roasted until it burned, then ground and simmered in hot water. Tortillas from the day before were warmed on the clay griddle.

"Let's go, son," Manuel slid his chair back and lifted his straw hat from a peg on the wall by the door.

Oscar found his hat, a miniature of his father's, as they went out the door.

"How many calves are there, Papa?" he asked as they started up the hill hand in hand.

"There were 10 the other day in the pasture where we're going. There'll probably be more by now. We need to see how they're all doing."

The boy was full of questions as they walked.

This ranch was Manuel's pride and joy. It was his life. He knew every foot of it, having walked it all himself. Over the years he gradually acquired neighboring properties until his holdings were impressive, and he was known as one of the most successful ranchers in the valley. His seven brothers had also established themselves on adjacent lands. Early on they decided to farm together as a cooperative business, and Manuel, being the eldest, was recognized as the head of the family firm.

He took justifiable pride in his ranch, but more than that, he loved it. He loved the open spaces, the green pastures, the streams, and he never failed to feed his soul with the picture of the mountains beyond. *I have everything I ever wanted*, he often thought.

The father and son trudged along the path, leading to the pasture where the cows with the new calves were kept. "There they are," Oscar shouted as they came over the brow of a hill. He ran on ahead. "Look! I see two new baby calves."

"Yes, and look over by those trees. Let's see how many we can find!" Manuel shared his son's excitement. They spent the next hour checking every cow and calf. Oscar was learning how to be a rancher.

"Oscar, come and help me!" The boy had wandered down by a stream. "We're going to move these cattle over the hill to another pasture."

The sun was getting low on the horizon when they finally headed back down the mountain toward home. Oscar turned toward his father. "I'm going to be a rancher when I grow up, and have lots of cows and lots of calves!"

Manuel smiled down at his son. "Well, learn all you can. I hope you'll be a good rancher." It was a tired but happy little boy that crawled into his bed that night.

Those happy days would forever live in Oscar's memory. Not only did his father teach him the ways of a cattleman on his ranch, but he taught him all the things about nature that he knew. He learned the names of the birds, and even to recognize their songs. He learned the names of the trees and wildflowers that grew on their ranch. Manuel had the same sensitive nature that his son had inherited, and they were truly kindred spirits. He was a good father to all his children, and all his sons took responsibility on the ranch, but this child—his last son—was special. The two became inseparable. Oscar knew that someday part of this big, beautiful ranch would be his.

One day after the evening meal and chores were finished, the older boys went to the home of their cousins, and the younger ones played in the nearby field. Although the twilights are short in the tropics, they are often brilliant. On this evening Manuel and Magdalena gravitated to their favorite place on the old fallen tree trunk in their front yard. To the east and north their land stretched up into the hills; to the west the road led to the distant village and the mountains beyond. The sky was vibrant with color. They sat there, drinking it all in, feeling the joy of working people who see the results of their labors. Manuel broke the silence. "I always dreamed of owning a farm like this. It is like a part of me. I feel so good to know that our children will have their future secure. This land will be theirs someday."

"We are so fortunate," Magdalena turned to him with her eyes shining. "You are a good provider, Manuel, and I am happy."

"Remember the days when your father thought you would starve if you married me?" Manuel laughed.

"How could I forget?" she replied. "But you'll have to say that he admitted his mistake, and when he learned to know you he treated you like a son."

"That is so true," her husband conceded. "And I

couldn't blame him for not liking me at first. My life didn't look too promising at that time. We really got to be good friends though, and I really miss the old man."

Her father had died, and the house in the village with part of his farmland had been willed to Magdalena and Manuel.

A little later Oscar came around the corner of the house and saw them sitting there. As he came closer he heard them singing. He often heard his mother sing, and he'd heard his father sing out on the range, but he never remembered hearing them sing together. He was too young to understand that the beautiful music he was hearing was sung in two parts. A phrase of the song stayed in his mind—"*Oh, Señor! Siempre escucha mi canto!*" The plaintive tune and words made a deep impression on the boy. He didn't know that it was a song his mother had learned as a child, the words and music almost becoming part of her. That night he went to bed, thinking of the beautiful harmony and the gripping words, "*Oh, Señor! Siempre escucha mi canto, Para siempre contigo estaré.*" ("Oh, Lord, forever hear my song, forever to be with Thee!")

As he grew, many times he saw and heard his parents singing that song together. In later years the plaintive melody seemed etched in his mind, connected with nostalgic childhood memories. It brought a certain comfort during the terrible time ahead.

Chapter 4

*I*t's time to round up the cattle from the far east section," Manuel told the group seated around the covered porch of his home. "The cattle buyers will be coming this next month." The eight brothers often gathered at Manuel's house to discuss plans for their cattle business.

Although their parents had died when the boys were young and after dividing the property eight ways none of them had much land, the brothers had a rich heritage of family values; respect for their elders, strong ties with each other, and loyalty to and pride in the Gomez name. Each of the eight brothers lived with his wife and children on his own land, but the business of the ranch was done together.

The nearest village, 17 kilometers to the west, served the area around it and was the last village on the only road leading into a mountain range. Beyond the rolling pasturelands of the Gomez brothers rose the mountains.

Darkness fell as the brothers talked about their plans for the cattle roundup, and the light of the candles flickered through the windows to the porch. Magdalena appeared at the door. "Oscar, it's time for you to come in. Little boys need to be in bed."

"I'm coming, Mama," the boy answered, "but first I have to know. Can I go with you to round up the cattle, Papa?"

The father smiled. "I might have known you would ask that. I'll talk it over with your mother. Maybe. Now run along to bed."

A few days later when Manuel strode out the gate toward the hills, Oscar was with him. His older brothers had joined some of their cousins and uncles. Each one knew his specific responsibility for that day, and which area of the range to search. But Oscar stayed close to his father. By midmorning they were herding the cattle back down the path that had been worn through the years by the Gomez stock. Although the morning air was crisp, the sun was out and Oscar shed his jacket. Manuel circled back and forth rounding up strays. Oscar did his part, running on the other side of the herd to help keep them together.

About midday they came to a green valley and found a small stream. The cattle headed for the water and, after drinking, began to graze in the luxuriant grass. "We'll stop here for a little rest, Oscar. Are you hungry?"

"*Sí, señor, tengo mucho hambre!*" ("Yes, sir, I am very hungry!")

They found an inviting spot in the shade of a tree, and spread out the cloth that covered their lunch. Pensively, Manuel began talking. "Someday this will all belong to you and your brothers, Oscar. You need to learn all you can about being a good rancher. Your uncles and I have worked hard to make the ranch what it is today. If you work together like we have, you can have a good life here too." Although the conversation had taken a serious turn—almost too serious for a 5-year-old boy—Oscar always remembered that day and his father's words. Perhaps it was the very seriousness of it that locked it into his mind.

The main corral for the Gomez cattle was located about half way between the village and Manuel's house and was central for the various family properties. When all the cattle from one of their range lands were herded into the fenced area, Manuel counted them. Then he and Oscar walked on home. The little boy was tired, but he would not admit it. It had been a long day for both of them, and they were hungry. They eagerly joined the rest of the family at the long table. A stack of tortillas wrapped in a clean cloth waited for them. A dish of beans, another of rice, and a kettle of stew made up their meal. The tortillas were made from the corn in their field. They'd grown the beans on their farm too. Beef, potatoes, carrots, onions, and chayote made up the stew. Most of their food was provided from their own ranch.

When all the children were in bed, Manuel sat at the table with his account books open before him. Maggie sat nearby with sewing in her hands. "This will be a good year for us, my dear," he told her. "The cattle are fat, and the prices will be good." He gave a satisfied sigh.

"You're a good rancher, Manuel, and you provide well for us. Many of the village people are poor. They haven't done so well."

"Of course we work hard," Manuel agreed, "but our

success is largely owing to the way we all work together. I'm glad that our family left us this tradition."

A few days later, Manuel and Francisco, one of his brothers, were out at the corral. "How many cattle did you say we brought down?" Francisco called to him.

"There were 76. I counted several times."

"Well, I can come up with only 72."

Manuel frowned. "It has been a long time since we've been bothered with cattle rustlers. Let's go and count them together."

They counted again. Four were missing, and on that day trouble began for the entire family. Cattle were missing on a regular basis.

Although their remote home was far from any heavily populated area, the Gomez family listened to news on their radio. On the rare occasions when someone went to the village, they brought back newspapers. Troubling information had been circulating for several months. Their country seemed to be in conflict, and some said it might turn into a civil war. Dissidents criticized the government, saying that it was not fair to the poor people. Some even thought that Communist leaders had infiltrated the country to spread discontent among the people.

When the army moved in and set up a base near their village, Manuel and his brothers feared that the political problems were coming close to them. Government authorities knew that revolutionaries usually set up headquarters in outlying areas. Rumors of such activity had prompted this latest action by the army.

One day a neighbor told Manuel that he'd been losing cattle. "Some people say that local beef is being sold cheap to the army," he told him.

Manual's brow was furrowed. "Is that so? Then we do have a problem. I've been missing cattle too."

"Do you think we should go and complain to the army?" the neighbor asked.

"I don't know, but I think that's one reason they're here, to protect people in this area." Manuel felt unsure, wondering what should be done.

"You know, Manuel, you're the biggest rancher around here," the man told him. "I think it will do more good if you go and talk to the commander."

"I'll pay him a visit," Manuel decided, and the two parted. His mood was troubled as he slowly walked toward home. He'd felt so safe and secure in the beautiful, isolated area of his home and vast ranch lands. Fear nipped his mind. *What is happening? Could the political problems we hear about have an effect on us?*

A few days later when Manuel stood before the commander's desk, he felt a certain aloofness. "What is your problem?" the commander asked curtly.

"We have cattle rustlers in our area," the rancher told him. "I've been losing cattle on a regular basis. Just in the last month, 10 head disappeared. I've been told that the army is buying their beef locally. I wonder if you would tell me who you are buying from."

"This is confidential information. I would suggest that you put some watchmen around your place." And with that, the commander picked up papers on his desk and began to read. The conversation was finished.

Manuel was miffed. Even if the army didn't know

who was stealing, he'd expected at least some interest on their part. Since setting up the base, the military had taken on somewhat of a policing image, and the people expected protection from them.

One morning about a week later Manuel went out to the corral, Oscar trailing along behind him as he often did. To their horror, one of their biggest steers was tied to a tree, wailing in pain. Coming closer, he saw that a huge slice of meat had been cut from the animal's side. Oscar was frightened as his father broke into tears.

"Who could have done such a thing? What is happening? Who is my enemy?" he cried.

Several more times they found cattle tied and mutilated. Watchmen were posted, but the evil perpetrators were never seen. Manuel and his family were devastated, confused, and frightened. He went to the commander again, but the man was cold and unconcerned. In the meantime, comments filtered through to him that confirmed in his mind that his stolen cattle were being sold to the army, and the culprits were being protected by them.

Manuel had no way of knowing—he could not imagine—that a sophisticated, sinister plan was under way by revolutionaries to turn the people and the army against each other.

Chapter 5

Manuel was worried. "I've been thinking," he told his wife. "We're really isolated out here at the ranch house, and every time I go into the village I hear about more problems. Other ranchers are losing cattle too. Besides that, the problems in the government are getting out of control. Even people are coming up missing." He paused, his face etched with concern. "I think we should move in with your mother in the village. It will be safer, especially when I am gone."

Although the grandma's house was bigger and better, the family preferred their home on the ranch. They'd lived there for many years and it was *home*. But Magdalena agreed with her husband. They would be safer in the village.

So several weeks later the Gomez family moved in with Grandma. This house was made of adobe bricks with a red tile roof. It had four bedrooms, a large living and eating area, and an attached kitchen at the back. It also boasted of the luxury of a bathroom—a room with a bathtub-shaped brick "box." They put coals in the box, made a fire, and when the bricks were hot, lifted out the coals. Water was then poured into the box, providing a sort of sauna. A large container of cold water and a dipper sat nearby. Thus one could take a cool shower as well as a steam bath.

While it was painful for Magdalena to leave the ranch, she enjoyed setting up housekeeping in her childhood home. Her mother was happy for the company, and Manuel could still attend to his cattle, since the corral was about the same distance as from the ranch house. Situated on the outskirts of the village, the house included an acreage where they could have gardens, animals, and a field of corn.

While working in the cornfield one morning, Manuel heard a rustling noise and looked up, coming face-to-face with a tall, blond man, who was armed. It was not unusual for the men in that area to carry machetes, but Manuel felt alarmed to be confronted with an armed stranger on his own property. It was obvious that this man was not one of his countrymen, for his people were of Mayan descent. When the stranger spoke, Manuel was surprised to hear his fluent Spanish.

"Buenos dias, Señor Gómez" ("Good morning, Mr. Gomez"), the stranger said politely.

"How do you know my name?" Manuel felt apprehensive. He'd never seen the man before.

"I have information. I know that you have been having a lot of problems with your cattle. Maybe I can help you."

Manuel couldn't hide his surprise. *Who is this stranger anyway?* he wondered. *One thing is certain—he is not from this area. Despite his good Spanish, I know he is a foreigner.*

The man took a piece of paper from his pocket. "I have two lists here. One is of those who have taken advantage of people and done a lot of damage. We call that our black list. The other is a list of farmers and others who have been mistreated. We want to help these people. Fortunately, you are on the last list. I know all about your problem. I'll help you and all your brothers if you'll help me."

Manuel looked the tall stranger in the eye. "Who are you anyway?"

"I am with the People's Army," he replied. Then noting the caution in Manuel's eyes, he added, "You've probably heard a lot of rumors, most of them spread by the army. The truth is that the People's Army is here to stop the corruption in the government. We are on the side of the people. Don't be afraid. We are here to help you."

Manuel listened to the man at length. His first inclination was to have nothing to do with him. But between the rancor he felt toward the army commander and his worry over the problem with the cattle, he knew he needed help. Listening to his persuasive words, Manuel wondered if joining this effort to change the government was truly the only solution. The stranger pressed his case. But Manuel hesitated. He would not make such a decision without discussing it with his family.

"I can't give you an answer yet," he said firmly.

"OK," the man said. "Talk it over with your brothers. I'll be here exactly two weeks from tonight. If you and your brothers are interested in joining us, be ready to leave with me. You can go and see our center for training and orientation, and then decide." With that the stranger was gone.

The next 14 days passed in a swirl of mental turmoil for Manuel. He'd heard about the revolutionaries—all enemies of the government. But the man had seemed sincere and convincing. Manuel dared to almost hope that this was the only solution to the problems of his people; that their cause was a just one, and they would be the winners.

One evening when all of the brothers were together at his house, Manuel told them of the strange visitor and his proposal. Some of his brothers were ready for help of any kind; others were fearful.

Pedro, next in age to Manuel, objected strenuously. "Do you realize what this could do to our families? You know that it's against the law to aid or abet any movement against the government!"

"I know, Pedro," Manuel agreed. "But this man says that the movement by the people is growing so strong that the army will be outnumbered. If we all unite in fighting the injustices, we can make a difference. In the end it will be better for everyone."

They talked until nearly midnight, each of the men expressing his concerns or interest. But they couldn't reach any conclusion.

Magdalena grew alarmed when Manuel discussed it with her. "How can you even *think* of cooperating with people fighting the government? Don't you know how dangerous that can be?"

He shook his head. "You may be right, but we have

to do something. It looks like the army is helping the criminals. They won't even listen to us."

Magdalena—contrary to her culture's custom—argued with her husband, pointing out problems inherent in the situation. But she knew that in the end she would accept whatever he decided, and she did have implicit confidence in him. Nevertheless, worry and apprehension haunted her days. It seemed impossible that the tranquillity and security she'd known such a short time before might be gone.

It was another matter to convince his brothers. They'd always worked together, and Manuel wouldn't go without them. They met together several evenings during those two short weeks, going over and over the stranger's plan.

The men objected when Manuel explained that if, after visiting the training camp, they decided to stay, they'd be away for several months. They couldn't leave their families alone. What about the finances? Who would support their wives and children?

"That won't be a problem," Manuel assured them. "The commander told me that if we join their army, our salaries will be enough to provide for our families."

Some of his brothers nodded. Others just shook their heads.

Then one morning they discovered several of their big steers brutally mutilated and five more missing. Naturally, they were frantic with worry. "It won't do any good to go to the army," Manuel told them, his face twisted in anger and desperation. "The commander of the People's Army says that the military is behind all of this."

The long and intense deliberations continued. Finally each of the brothers reluctantly agreed that they should at least find out what the People's Army was all about. It wouldn't hurt to go and visit their camp. There seemed to be no other choice.

Tension filled Manuel's home as the day neared when the stranger would return. But Manuel could not forget the army officer's cold attitude when he'd reported missing and mutilated cattle. The more Manuel thought of the insult to him—a well-known land owner—the more determined he became to consider the stranger's offer.

On that evening, just two weeks after they'd met, Manuel knelt down and talked to little Oscar. "There'll be a visitor here tonight, but you are to stay in your room. Do you understand?"

Oscar nodded solemnly.

"I have to be gone for a while," his father continued, "but you'll be safe here with your mother and brothers. I'll be back before long."

Oscar stayed in bed but could not sleep.

Manuel and his brothers were waiting in the shadows of the porch. And at the precise moment he'd promised, the man—actually the captain of the guerrillas—arrived. Manuel felt a stab of fear. All kinds of rumors about the revolutionaries whirled around the village and countryside. *What are we getting ourselves into?* he wondered, but he pushed the thoughts aside. He could see no other choice.

When Oscar heard voices outside, he peeked through the window and saw a big, tall man talking to his father. The little fellow had overheard serious conversations between his parents, and he sensed their tension. And now this secret meeting outside at such a late hour seemed ominous. He stood at the window for a long minute, troubled and fearful. But then, trusting his father, he crawled back in bed and finally slept.

Manuel's fears were soon put aside by the disarming manner of the leader. He was more than friendly, assuring the Gomez brothers that their problems could soon be over, and that they could be valuable soldiers to the revolutionary movement.

So strong and convincing were the captain's arguments that Manuel and his brothers agreed to go with him to one of the rebel camps for orientation and training. Manuel came back into the house to tell Magdalena. "Listen, we've decided to go with him," he began. Her dark eyes grew wide with alarm, and he touched her arm to comfort her. "Don't worry. It will be all right."

"But, Manuel, how long will you be gone?"

"I'm not sure, and they can't tell us where we are going. But I'll come back as soon as I can. Now I need you to help me pack just what's necessary, just what I can carry on my back."

Silently, mechanically, Magdalena began collecting a few items for her husband. Tears spilled from her eyes onto her cheeks.

At the last minute, Manuel's chest tightened in a panic that almost changed his mind. But the die had been cast. They would go. If they angered the rebel captain, the rebels might become their enemies, and he well knew that this might prove the worst danger of all.

The sun arose next morning as always, but the house seemed dark and cold. The family tried to act as if everything were the same, but a heavy gloom reached into every corner of their home. The children had been told that their father would be gone for a while, but none of them guessed that it would be a year before they even heard from him again.

For the first few days, Oscar didn't know what to do with himself. He just aimlessly wandered around the house and yard, his mind far, far away. It didn't seem right that his father would leave without him. A sense of trouble hung over the whole family, but, mercifully, none of them could foresee that the happy life they'd known was at an end.

Chapter 6

Magdalena and the children kept things going as normally as possible, but she lived in deadly fear that someone would find out that her husband was with the revolutionaries. As the weeks went by she realized that he and his brothers must have decided to accept the help of the People's Army and join them. It was hard to explain his long absence to the children and to the neighbors. Her only comfort was to whisper her concerns with the wives of the other brothers. The women kept the fearful secret among themselves.

Day after day she hoped and waited for some word from Manuel. She had no idea where he was or just what he was doing, only that it had to do with rebels who planned to overthrow the government, promising a bright future for them all.

Magdalena had learned to weave and embroider when she was a young girl, and as the weeks slipped into months her weaving helped pass the time. The women in her village and the surrounding area wore the typical woven skirt and blouse. In fact, one could know what village a woman was from by the colors in her dress. The skirts Magdalena and the other women wore were made of a finely woven length of red material with white stripes. They simply wound the long length of material around their hips and legs, securing it at the waist with a stiff, woven belt.

Their blouses boasted handwoven designs of various colors. The handwork was so intricate that one blouse could take weeks or even months to make, and each one was the pride of the wearer. A bright, woven shawl completed the outfit. The shawl could be used for warmth, or wrapped over the shoulder around and under one arm to provide a carryall for a baby. In some cases, the shawl was simply folded and carried over one shoulder. From the tiniest little girl to the oldest grandma, the dress was of the same style and colors, the only difference being in the condition and age of the garment. Although the natural dyes were very good, years of washing made some garments more faded and dingy.

Magdalena always wore skirts and blouses that were new and bright, especially when she appeared in public. She tied her long shining black hair at the nape of her neck with a colorful ribbon. Besides making all of her own clothes, she often wove beautiful tapestries and tablecloths for her own home, and to sell. Foreign visitors often found her remote village and were entranced with the picturesque countryside and colorful village life. When Magdalena went to the market, Oscar and his sisters went along. Market day was an important part of village life.

"When is my papa coming home?" Oscar often asked

his mother. The boy couldn't understand why his father—who always before had taken him with him—would stay away so long. "Where is he? What is he doing?"

"Your father had some important business, son," she would answer. "I'm sure he'll be coming back one of these days soon."

The months dragged by one after another. The children grew accustomed to their father's absence, and Oscar found other boys in the village to play with that took the place of the time he'd spent with his father. But with each passing day Magdalena's worry increased. At last a year had passed. Twelve long months. She could never have imagined Manuel would be away so long. Where was he? What was he doing?

Then late one night Manuel and his brothers returned. Each one was heavily armed. To her dismay, Magdalena learned that they'd spent months in the guerrilla camp and were now trained as full-fledged revolutionaries. Strangely, sadly, having her husband back in their home didn't bring the comfort Magdalena had expected. He was back, but he was different.

They talked far into the night, their voices mere whispers in the darkness. It was not safe for Manuel and his brothers to linger in the village. Rumors could spread. Someone might suspect where they'd been, and no one knew where the sympathies of a person were—with the military or with the People's Army. By then the military was aware that the guerrillas had infiltrated that area, and their main mission was to search them out.

"Tomorrow we are sending all of you—every one in our family—up to a safe place. It's where we've been all this time. The place is so fortified that no one can even find it, let alone get in there alive."

No! Magdalena thought. "No," she whispered. "No."

But Manuel hushed her fears. "Don't worry," he murmured. "You will be safe. And other women and children are there. There are tents, too, where we can live. Someone will be here to lead the way and my brothers and I will be along in a few days. We must see to the cattle first."

"But I don't want to go, Manuel. Why can't I still stay on here?"

She struggled to grasp the jolting news that she must leave her home. Her *home.* But there was something more. Magdalena sensed that this was not the same man she'd fallen in love with and lived with those many years. She had no way of knowing or comprehending the intense training and mind control that he and his brothers had been subjected to. Although they doubtless feared they'd made a terrible mistake, to turn back now—with all the knowledge of the rebels that they possessed—would mean certain death to both them and their families. They were in a nightmarish trap with no way out. But Manuel had to try to quiet his wife's fears.

"You don't realize that things are getting worse every day," he told her. "There's going to be a fight with the army, and you and the children cannot stay here. We'll come back when things get better," Manuel assured her. "This is an organized army we are joining. They have a well-equipped camp, and they're prepared to defend it. We can't stay here at the mercy of these bandits."

With horrible foreboding and many tears Magdalena picked out the things they'd need most. She'd always supported Manuel and had taught the children to respect and obey him. This would be no different.

So while the children slept, their parents prepared to leave their village home without arousing suspicion. They packed into bundles what Magdalena and the children could carry on the three-day trip. They would walk all the way, and must pack carefully. They'd need food, what clothing they could carry, and bedding.

Each one of Manuel's brothers was doing the same thing in his own home, preparing their families to trek up into the mountains. It was a hurried process. So that their going would be unnoticed, they needed to leave before daylight. They'd go in small groups so no attention would be noted of their leaving. They left what they couldn't carry in their houses and locked the doors. All hoped that the problems would soon be over and they could return home. But none knew if, in reality, they would ever be back.

Although her mother objected, Magdalena insisted that she come too. Naturally, the woman didn't want to leave her home and friends. But it would not be safe to leave her alone. In the end she gave in. Grandmother, too, would join her family in the walk to the camp in the mountains.

Oscar and his brothers had been asleep when their father arrived the night before, but their parents awoke them early. Magdalena calmly and confidently explained to the children that they needed to leave quickly. At first Oscar was overjoyed to see his father.

But when he learned that the family was leaving on a trip to the mountains and his father was not going with them, he refused to go.

"No!"

He planted his feel firmly on the floor and looked from his mother to his father. "I am staying with Papa." Manuel tried to reason with him, but he would not budge. His reaction was so strong that at last Manuel relented. In that early-morning hour they could not have the noise of a crying boy.

"All right. You can stay, but I'm telling you that it won't be easy," Manuel said. "You have to promise me that you won't cry no matter what happens." He then turned to his wife. "We will follow you in two weeks."

Then it was time for them to leave. Oscar watched silently as the family quietly crept away. In all, about 90 members of the Gomez family left in the predawn darkness with only what they could carry. When they were beyond the view of the village, the different families met at a prearranged place and traveled together.

Manuel and Oscar left for the ranch as soon as the rest of the family was gone. They needed to make arrangements for care for the cattle while they were away. Six-year-old Oscar felt confused and sad, but he was with his father, and that was most important to him.

Manuel and his brothers met at the corral to check out the cattle. They needed to find out how many were missing and if bandits still stole and mutilated the animals. It didn't take them long to learn from the older boys who'd been left to care for them that cattle were still missing.

They'd brought bedrolls and food and took turns sleeping at the corral so they could determine the pattern the bandits followed. Before they returned to their village they'd decided on a plan of revenge on the bandits.

One night the guerrilla captain came to see the Gomez men. They stood in a circle around him to hear what he had to say. "First of all, we need to catch the thieves," he told them. "They're probably stooges of the army. Now that you know when they'll be coming and how they are working we'll set a trap." He turned to Manuel. "The strategy will be this: I will bring some of my men, and we'll surround the corral. We'll give the bandits time to get in and get started. And at a signal, we'll come down on them."

On that terrible, unforgettable night about 500 guerrillas gathered at the far end of the corral. The tall, blond captain was in charge. "You Gomez brothers stay near me. The rest of you encircle the corral but stay out of sight."

Lights from a generator had been placed at strategic points in the corral. A flick of a switch would turn them on.

The men waited in silence. Suddenly they heard footsteps, and a large number of bandits armed with machetes slipped into the corral and began slaughtering the cattle. Manuel and his brothers waited breathlessly for the captain to give the signal. Oscar had been told to stand back out of sight, but he edged up close enough to see what was happening.

Abruptly the lights flashed on and the captain shouted, *"Manos arriba!"* ("Hands up!") "Put down your arms!" he commanded. "No one will leave here alive."

Terrified, the bandits dropped their machetes to the ground.

"Here is the family that has been affected by your thieving," the captain called to them. At that, the eight Gomez brothers stepped forward. "You have tied the cattle to trees to kill them. Now these men will tie you to trees."

The bandits began to plead for mercy, giving names of others who had been implicated. Coldly, silently, the captain wrote the names on his list.

Then the large guerrilla army descended on the bandits, helplessly tied to trees. In the terrible confusion Manuel forgot about his little son standing in the background, witnessing the carnage. The boy wanted to cry out, but he forced the scream back into his chest. Bile heaved into his throat. He needed to vomit, but he'd promised his father he would be brave—no matter what happened.

When it was over, the corral was strewn with bodies. Not one of the bandits escaped. The ruthless guerrilla army tossed the dead into a pile and set them on fire. Then they hurriedly left for the mountains.

Chapter 7

*I*t took three days for the men and young boy to reach the camp. They crossed rivers, climbed over huge boulders, went through thick woods, and finally, climbing almost a perpendicular rock wall, arrived at the camp in a forest so dense that the sun could barely penetrate the trees.

They arrived just before dark on the third day, and Manuel went to the headquarters to learn where to find his family. Oscar trailed along, looking at the rows and rows of tents. "Is Mama here?" he asked his father, clinging to his hand. It all seemed so strange.

"Yes, she and the rest of the family are here. We'll soon find them." Finally, walking down to the far end where the new arrivals were housed, they found the right tent.

"Manuel! I'm so glad you're here at last!" Magdalena felt relieved and happy to see her husband and son. Each tent was designed to sleep two people, so sitting on the two cots they caught up on what had happened since they'd parted. "I was concerned for your safety," Magdalena told him, blinking back tears of relief. "I don't know what I would have done if you hadn't showed up."

Manuel told his wife about the execution at the corral. "It was terrible," he confided. "I'm not a fighter by nature, and I don't like this business. But those men only got what they deserved." He nodded toward Oscar, who had fallen asleep on one of the cots. "But I'm sorry the little fellow was there. I shouldn't have let him stay."

"Do you mean that Oscar witnessed *that?*"

"I told him to stay back out of sight, but in all the excitement I forgot about him. Evidently he got curious when it all erupted. I'm sorry, Maggie."

She sighed. It was just one more frightening, puzzling piece of their new life. And it couldn't be changed.

Later she showed Manuel the tents assigned to their family. Oscar would sleep in the tent next to theirs with one of his older brothers. The tents were only equipped for sleeping. Everyone in the camp ate under a big canopy at one of the large dining tents.

They soon learned that everyone—men, women, and children—was assigned duties. The women took care of the domestic chores, but some of them, especially the younger ones, received the same combat training as the men. These women and girls wore the same drab olive uniforms that the men wore. They piled their hair up under the caps. All of the men were trained in different units of combat.

During the day all children age 5 and older were taken to a separate area for special training. The younger ones were taught to go into the villages to make purchases and to listen for information. They were drilled daily in the tactics of secrecy and loyalty to the revolution. This training was designed to brainwash them to the point where they would never give out information, no matter what was done to them. It was an intense mental discipline and brain control.

Oscar soon adjusted to the program. There were short periods of recreation, and he made friends with other children, returning to his family only for mealtime and sleeping.

The camp was a city in itself, meticulously set up for a long civil war. The 3,000 or so simple country people gathered there were awed by the sophistication of the complex. There were underground tunnels, electronic equipment, a communication system, and large caches of arms. There was an electric plant and enough barrels of diesel and other supplies to support the city. Everything was highly organized. The camp leaders were foreigners like the commander who had come to Manuel's house.

Although the camp was a long walk from the nearest village and supplies, a system was carefully worked out. That's where the younger children came in. On their "market days," adults would go with the children to one of the villages, but stay back out of sight. The carefully trained children went into the village, nonchalantly buying supplies and loitering around to hear whatever news they could. Then they joined the adults at the edge of town and arranged their packs for the trip back. As the children became more adept at their jobs they were given more responsibility.

Older children worked as guards. The camp was arranged with four strategic corners. Each one had a guard day and night. Those on duty knew how to give the signals of warning if any stranger approached.

After a year Oscar spent his days with a group of children in another nearby camp getting advanced training. He often went to one of the villages to buy supplies. He'd circulate around the village, and especially around any military personnel, listening and learning all he could. At times he'd overhear soldiers talking about certain maneuvers or plans of attack. Sometimes they boasted of victories—so many guerrillas captured or killed—and sometimes they talked of devastating attacks on the military. Since the guerrilla army had chosen these isolated mountain areas for their centers of operation and hideouts, the military also moved into the area. At times fierce fighting ensued.

On one occasion Oscar went to a village with several other children and an adult. The children scattered when they arrived. Since he was small for his age, Oscar could loiter around without being noticed, and he saw two soldiers talking at the corner of a building. Nonchalantly, he went just around the corner where he could hear their conversation, and sat down in the dirt, playing with some rocks.

"I just heard on our radio that another bridge has been blown up by these blasted terrorists!" he heard one of the soldiers say.

"If we could just know where their hideout is," the other replied. "You never know when you'll step on a mine or have a grenade thrown at you. I wonder if this conflict will ever end."

The little boy playing in the dirt took it all in to report to the man waiting for him up the hill from the village.

When Oscar was 7 he joined a training class with other boys his age to carry and use arms. Everyone at the camp was taught that the military was the ultimate enemy. Everything possible was done to hassle and destroy the army. The training and orientation were so planned as to completely convince the people to believe that they were doing their country a service. Learning to shoot was a game for the children. Oscar became such an astute student that the guerrilla leaders singled him out as a potential leader. The loyalty and obedience he'd once given his parents were transferred to the guerrilla teachers and soldiers.

Manuel and the other men spent a lot of time away from the camp carrying out the orders of the leaders, wreaking havoc on military troops, blowing up bridges, and keeping the soldiers in confusion and panic. The Claymore bombs they used were made at the camp. Magdalena began to see her husband as a different person—withdrawn, intense, angry, and nervous. The indoctrination had changed him from the mild, gentle man she'd always known. She was concerned about the future of her family, but she herself had been sent to training classes designed to bend her mind and loyalties to the goals of the revolution. Besides, she well knew that to abandon the camp would be deadly. She and her family knew too much. They would be hunted by the guerrillas as well as the military.

Then Oscar and some of his friends moved to another camp—the Action Camp—for advanced training.

It was closer to town, and they concentrated on methods of attacking and molesting the military.

Until then he'd lived with his family at one of the family camps, part of the main camp. He was reluctant to leave, but he'd made friends among other boys. And camp leaders made him feel important for having been chosen for advanced training. It was an honor for an 8-year-old boy.

These young boys, these *children*, learned to be real sharp shooters. On one forage to the village a helicopter hovered over them. Together, they shot it down. Whenever they were successful in doing harm to the enemy they were praised as heroes for the revolution.

In the evenings social events kept the boys entertained and content. Sometimes there were slide shows. No matter what the activity, it had the intent of increasing their loyalty and interest in overthrowing the government.

One day a group of them were on the hill just above an army base. They threw a grenade bomb at the quarters, but it hit a light post and glanced off to a football field where a group of soldiers were having a party. Apparently all were killed.

"We've got to get out of here!" Oscar hissed to the others. The boys ran for the hills.

Occasionally Oscar longed for their ranch and the carefree life they used to have, but such moments were brief. Camp leaders kept the boys so busy, and so inflamed with the passion of winning the war and becoming heroes, that they had little time for reflection. And they had no choice but to follow orders.

It *was* possible to leave the camp. But anyone who did knew that his or her very life depended on absolute silence in regard to any knowledge of the guerrillas. If caught, nothing—including the threat of death—was to persuade them to divulge any information. Combined with the threat of retribution, instilled in each was a strong sense of loyalty and honor.

One day a man stated his desire to leave. He had good reasons, and his loyalty was not questioned. Little did anyone realize what the consequences would be to the entire camp.

Chapter 8

One day the commander in charge of camp security called Oscar to headquarters. "You have proved yourself trustworthy. We have decided that you can take a shift as guard. Do you think you can stay awake if I put you on one of the night shifts?"

Oscar straightened up with pride. This was an honor for a boy not quite 9 years old. "Yes, sir, I think I can."

With his training period finished at the Action Camp, Oscar had joined the rest of the family back at the main camp. In spite of his age, the leaders had singled him out as one they could trust with responsibility. The grown men were used in the active guerrilla army, striking the military in surprise attacks at strategic points. The idea was to keep the army in confusion and demoralize it. To discredit the army, attacks were often made on civilians in such a way as to place the blame on the army, even going so far as to give the guerrilla soldiers uniforms taken from the bodies of military men they had killed. In the skirmishes between the army and the guerrillas, innocent villagers were often caught in the cross fire. It was no secret that any civilian sheltering or aiding the rebels would be dealt with the same as the guerrillas.

After working with another guard for a few nights, Oscar was assigned a night shift on certain nights of the week. His instructions were simple but specific. The posts were at the four corners of the camp. A shelter, protected from the weather, was situated so that a clear view could be seen in three directions. Everyone in camp knew that if a certain alarm sounded—touched off by a button at one of the watch points—everyone was to flee at once through designated openings in the trees onto paths leading down the mountain. Detailed plans of escape were mapped out.

During the three years that the Gomez family had been at the camp, the alarm had never gone off except in a trial exercise. Oscar had been so thoroughly trained and disciplined that he was not afraid to be alone at his post, but the inactivity was boring. Sometimes in the middle of the night he had to fight sleep.

Then came that fateful night. Oscar sat at the plain wooden table in the shelter, listening for any unusual noise. He walked out occasionally, looking and listening each way over the valley below, but all he heard were the jungle noises of little animals and the wind in the trees. When he sat down again, exhaustion combined with boredom overcame him, and resting his head on his arms, he fell asleep.

Suddenly the emergency alarm sounded! He sat up, electrified, but momentarily confused, trying to figure out which direction the alarm came from. He knew the secret escape route, but in his confusion he lost his sense of direction. Instead of running toward the secret opening in the dense foliage, he raced around in circles. Soon he heard the sound of boots coming through the trees, and the hushed voices of soldiers. He didn't know which way to run, and soon realized that he was surrounded. But they hadn't seen him yet. Suddenly his eyes pierced the darkness, and he recognized a large clump of tree roots. He knew that within them was an opening to a small cave under the roots that he and some other boys had discovered. He slipped in just in time, and a group of soldiers walked by. He was close enough to hear their hushed conversation.

"That informer described this place. I'm sure we have followed his map. I hope he hasn't sent us into a trap!"

Another voice answered, "If this is the place, we'll soon find the camp. Everything seems quiet. If they're here, everyone must be asleep."

Oscar trembled with fear. For the moment he seemed safe in his hiding place because the soldiers hadn't seen him, but what should he do? From their conversation he knew that a large company of soldiers had invaded the camp. He hoped that all of his family had escaped. Could he be the only one left behind?

The soldiers circled the camp and found it empty, though it was obvious that it was inhabited. So they set up a circle around the camp to watch for anyone trying to return. When the voices of the soldiers moved farther away, Oscar stole out of his hiding place. By now he had figured out where he was. His main thought was to find a way out of this trap. He knew where strategic mines had been placed in case of attack, and his first objective was to disconnect them so he could escape wherever there was an opening. He discovered that the army was still close by, and as the sun began to come up, he went back to his hiding place under the roots.

Listening for any sound, he decided that the soldiers must have withdrawn, and cautiously ventured out to assess the situation. But a new terror drove him back into hiding. Helicopters were circling the camp, and they began to bomb specific targets. The mountain shook with each explosion. Crouched in his cave, Oscar trembled with terror. His mind raced, searching for some plan that would allow him to escape. Then he remembered a subterranean room where arms were stored, and where the sophisticated electronic systems that controlled the camp were located. He determined that when darkness came and the bombing ceased for the night, he would search for the underground room. He knew that the room held a control that would set off explosions all around the camp. He had been there once, watching the commander in charge and listening to instructions given to another guerrilla.

When night came again, Oscar ventured out and discovered that the camp seemed to be abandoned. He found one of the arms caches—another cave where cannons, machine guns, hand grenades, and ammunition were stored. In his desperation he considered killing himself. *I'd rather kill myself than be captured,* he thought. But, although not completely discarding the idea, he decided to go back to his cave and sleep. Each person in the camp was taught to keep two days' provisions close by. His supply was in a knapsack on his back, but he knew that he must find a way out soon.

The third night he searched again. He knew that there were 10-foot ditches on the sides of the camp. Sharp sticks at the bottom would cut or stab anyone who fell in or tried to cross them unaware. Toward dawn Oscar crept toward one of the ditches. He was wondering if he should try to escape that way when he heard a cry. Two soldiers patrolling that area had fallen in one of the ditches. Oscar wondered if they would get out alive. He retreated again to his little cave.

The fourth night, driven by hunger and desperation, the boy determined he must find a way out. Again he ventured toward one of the ditches. He knew that a mountain stream with a waterfall lay below. He succeeded in going farther than he had before, but the terrain was rugged. Climbing over the side of the cliff, he grabbed a rock—and it moved. To his delight, he found that he'd discovered the underground headquarters, so using the flashlight he carried in his pack, he began to explore the large room. He saw a diagram of the whole camp, indicating the strategic points, including the automatic cannons hidden in different places. He found the light switch connected to batteries, and when he pulled it the whole place lit up. To his relief, he found some food rations. Then he examined the buttons connecting the automatic cannons, and he pushed some of them. Suddenly the whole camp erupted with explosions!

The army camped nearby went into action. But they were confused. Bombs were going off in different places, but not one person could be found. Oscar had thought he could drive the army away with the bombing, but it only reinforced their determination to discover the source. He felt safe in the underground room carved into solid rock, but he realized that he couldn't stay there forever. And he dared not venture out.

The next day he heard nothing—all seemed quiet. By now he was desperate to get out of his prison, so he slowly crept out, looking every direction. By late afternoon he decided that the army had withdrawn, and again he started toward the ditch and the river beyond. He crawled down into the ditch and went to its end toward the trees and the river.

Then he looked back and was filled with cold terror! A soldier stood on the bank with his rifle pointed in his direction! Oscar seemed paralyzed with fear. The soldier fired just as Oscar dropped down. But in falling, his right arm was raised and the bullet tore into the flesh.

In spite of the searing pain, the boy fled along the bottom of the ditch and then into the trees. When he reached the waterfall, he was seized by another fear. He'd never learned to swim very well, but his desperation was so great that he preferred drowning to being captured. He jumped into the water, and the current carried him downstream to where the water flowed more quietly. What a relief it was to feel solid ground beneath his feet, and he stumbled to the rocky, sandy shore. His arm was bleeding profusely, and he had to tend to that. He had an extra shirt in his knapsack. It would serve for a bandage, so he tied it around his arm the best he could.

Oscar was well acquainted with every part of the mountain, and he knew his way down. Although he was trained to do things that only a man should do, and take responsibilities that only a man should have, he was still a young boy—and he wanted to go home. The camp had been taken over by the army, much of it destroyed. He couldn't go back there. He hoped that his family had escaped, but even if they had, he had no idea where they were. His only thought was of his home. Maybe he'd find someone there. So he trudged down the mountain. He'd lost a lot of blood, but the bleeding had subsided. The pain was intense, but his training helped him to be brave.

He walked cautiously around the mountain for hours, always scanning the area for cover in case the army still pursued him. Finally, tired, hungry, and weak from the loss of blood, he came onto a path leading down the mountain. He decided to head for one of the camps on his father's ranch. It was used by the men during the cattle drives. Just maybe some of his family might be there.

Although tired and weak, the thought of home spurred him on. He tried to run, then walk, stumbling along. The hours passed, and night came on. He found a shelter behind some bushes, and exhausted, curled up on the ground with his knapsack for a pillow and fell asleep. At the break of dawn he got up, trying to remember where he was. Soon he found the path again and hurried on, weak and hungry, but the thought of possibly finding his family urged him on.

That afternoon he came over a knoll. Suddenly his heart beat with emotion as he realized that in the distance he could see his father's farm. With renewed energy he ran on. Finally he rounded a corner, looked down into the valley, and saw the cabin where he'd often stayed with his father. Even from that distance he could see someone in the yard. "My family is there!" he exclaimed in excitement. He could hardly wait and ran even faster. The path took a sharp turn around a small hill, and suddenly he stopped short. He was face-to-face with a soldier!

"Where are you going?" the soldier demanded.

"I'm going home. I live down there," Oscar answered. The soldier let him by. But as he rounded the last curve approaching the cabin, his heart nearly stopped.

Chapter 9

*T*he yard was filled with people, many, many people, and among them were soldiers. Oscar realized with horror that the army was there. He hoped he could get close without being noticed.

As he crept closer he realized that there were two lines of people in the yard. He saw members of his family in the lines. He saw his *father* at the end of the line. At that moment—when he was trying to comprehend what was happening—a soldier roughly grabbed him by the shoulder and pushed him into line with the rest of his family. There were no welcoming shouts of greeting from his family, just an ominous silence. Then he saw that across the yard there was another line—a line of soldiers. A captain stood between the lines, giving orders.

Soon the horrible truth dawned on Oscar. One by one, a soldier with a machete in his hand was ordered to pull the next person out of the line and take him or her into the cabin. Moments afterward, as if frozen in a nightmare, he saw blood running out of the doorway. After each victim went in, Oscar heard a piercing scream or cry. No one resisted. No one tried to escape. They knew the penalty for joining revolutionary forces. They thought they were fighting for their land and their rights, but they knew that someone would be the loser. A state of numbness, of unreality, pervaded the group.

But the children—when jerked away from their parents—cried and screamed with fear. "Mommy!" they shrieked, straining to get back to their mothers. "No! No!" they shouted at the soldiers. The helpless mothers could only turn their anguished faces and tear-filled eyes away.

Oscar numbly stood in line. A complete sense of unbelief and unreality blanked out the terror and fear that had first possessed him. Looking down the line of victims, he saw his cousins, aunts, and uncles. He saw his older brothers. He'd arrived in time to see Teresita taken by a soldier. He turned his head away. Frantically he looked up and down the line for his mother or his other sisters. *They're already dead!* he thought. He felt as if he would vomit or faint. Only the merciful numbness of shock kept him upright, and he covered his eyes with his hands.

Finally, his uncle—just in front of him—was taken into the cabin. Oscar covered his eyes. He knew he was next. But if all his family were murdered, he didn't want to live either. He felt as if he were already dead. There had been times up on the mountain when he wished he could die. Now he had no more feeling or emotion left.

The dreaded moment came. The captain pulled him out of line. But instead of handing him over to the next soldier, the man pushed him to one side and reached for the next victim.

Oscar stood back, watching, his mind spinning. The hardness and cruelty of the soldiers was beyond belief. A little boy, 4 or 5 years old, not realizing what was happening, ran up to his mother, saying, *"Tengo hambre!"* ("I'm hungry.")

A soldier grabbed the child and with a sneer, snarled *"Hambre, huh?"* ("Hungry, huh?") and strung him up to a nearby tree.

When the executions were complete, Oscar knew that his family, his uncles, aunts, cousins, as well as his own mother, sisters, and brothers were dead. Then he thought, *What happened to Papa? I saw him at first, but they didn't kill him.* Evidently, when everyone's attention was drawn to Oscar as he arrived, Manuel had slipped away. When the last victim was taken into the house, only Oscar remained. The captain turned to him. "Tie his hands behind his back!" he ordered a soldier. Then facing Oscar, he began, "Now, boy, you have been spared for one purpose and that is to tell us where the rest of these rebels are. Where is your father?"

"I don't know," Oscar answered, his eyes on the ground. Already a strong resolve was forming in his mind. *They can do what they want to me. I'll never tell them anything!* Anger and bitterness filled his chest, rose into his throat until he thought he would choke. He couldn't talk. He wouldn't. *What does it matter what happens to me?* he thought. *My whole family is gone. I don't even want to live!*

"So you don't want to talk, huh?" the captain said, looking with steely eyes at the defenseless boy.

Oscar did not reply.

Turning to a soldier, the captain ordered, "Get some

of those Claymore bombs and tie them on his back. Then we'll see if he'll talk!"

Eight of the bombs were tied onto his back. Their weight could hardly have been carried by a healthy, strong boy, and Oscar had spent days with almost no food. He had trudged miles coming down from the mountain. He staggered under the heavy bombs, his throbbing arm drenched with blood. However, he was not a coward, and he was determined not to let these cruel men intimidate him. He straightened up, trying to appear strong.

The sun sank down behind the mountain, and night was falling fast. The captain ordered his troop—the approximately 80 men who'd just performed the carnage on the Gomez family—to prepare to march. They would head for the mountains.

As they began their march, the captain confided to his second in command, "This boy is our only hope of finding the rest of this band. We have intelligence that there are several thousand of them. Their leaders are highly trained, and they have sophisticated weapons. They are the ones who have been blowing up bridges, attacking army troops, and wreaking havoc in the villages. They are turning all these villages against the army! My orders from the top general are to find their new headquarters and annihilate them!"

They marched until midnight. Although Oscar was near complete exhaustion, he would not give anyone the satisfaction of knowing it. When camp was set up for the night, the captain came to him. He seemed to be taking a new approach.

"I see something happened to your arm; let's take a look." He took off the bloody shirt and gasped at the ugly wound. "A bullet got you. Right?" Still the boy remained silent. The captain continued, "That's an ugly wound. We need to take care of it before it gets infected." Turning to one of his men, he ordered, "Get the first-aid case. We need to take care of this gunshot wound."

The captain cleaned and bandaged the wound, and Oscar asked himself, *After all he did, why does he care about my arm?*

And to himself, the man thought, *This boy had to have come from that camp up on the hill. He knows a lot of things we need to know.*

Chapter 10

*T*he next morning, after giving the order to prepare to march again, the captain came to Oscar. "You know, kid, these bombs on your back were set to go off in 24 hours. That will be this afternoon. If you get behind us, that will be tough for you. But all you have to do is tell us what you know and we'll take the bombs off and let you go. What do you say?"

Oscar only looked at the ground and said nothing. The captain gave the order to march, and they were off toward the mountain. Oscar had no idea where they were going. The load on his back was unbearably heavy, and with his hands tied behind him it was hard to keep his balance, especially on the rough terrain. The soldiers seemed to be deliberately trying to leave him behind, but his jaw was set. *They will not get away from me! If I die, they will all die with me!* The fact was, with his family dead, he had no desire to live. Death would be almost welcome. And so he gritted his teeth with determination, and he kept up the pace, no matter how fast the soldiers went. At times they broke into a trot. Difficult as it was, Oscar trotted too.

When they stopped for lunch, they tried other tactics. One of them asked, "Do you want to stay alone or do you want us to kill you?"

"Kill me!" he answered without flinching.

Oscar's hands were untied while he ate, and he saw that they were purple from lack of circulation. The captain pulled out a picture of his father. At the sight of the picture his heart gave a lurch. What had happened to his beloved father? One of the soldiers put a gun to his head. "Is this your father?" he asked.

In almost a whisper the boy answered, *"Sí."* ("Yes.")

"Where is your father?" the captain demanded.

"No sé." ("I don't know.")

Finally, late in the afternoon, an hour before the bombs were to go off, the captain gave the order, "Let him loose." He saw that they could not intimidate Oscar with the bombs and that he was not ready to talk.

Once the bombs were removed from his back, the whole troop, with Oscar behind, broke into a run. They ran on up the hill, making as much distance between them and the bombs as possible. Suddenly they heard a tremendous explosion, and a black cloud filled the area. "There she went!" someone shouted. The captain ordered them back to assess the damage, and they found a huge crater with the trees surrounding it uprooted. The captain turned to Oscar, "Do you see what could have happened to you? Now where are the rest of your band?"

"No sé," the boy answered without emotion. *"Mátame! Que tengo en este mundo? Han matado a toda mi familia!"* ("Kill me! What do I have left in this world.

You have killed my whole family!") At the last words, his voice broke.

That was the beginning.

For a month and a half, the band of soldiers and their captain marched and camped in the mountains, putting constant pressure on Oscar in whatever way they could imagine. But to all of their questions he only answered, *"No sé."*

With every passing sunrise and sunset his anger, bitterness, and depression deepened. He longed to die. But to the captain and his troop, he maintained a noncommittal stance. They could get nothing out of him. It was as if his small body were without feeling. There was nothing in his mind but anger, desperation, and a passion for revenge.

Finally, the troop was ordered to turn toward a distant village. Coming down from the mountain, they passed by a small settlement. "This is another place that has been friendly to the rebels," the captain remarked, and he gave the order to burn all the homes. In one of them, the family was shut inside and burned alive. The soldiers ravaged the whole area, killing men, women, and children. "This whole area is full of rebels!" they shouted. Cattle and chickens were stolen to be used for food. In one village the guerrillas had already burned half of the homes. The captain and his men burned the other half.

They were gradually working their way back to the military headquarters, and the closer they got, the more frustrated the captain seemed to be. He must face the hard-nosed commander who'd given him his orders.

And he was coming back with nothing to report.

A few miles before reaching the base, the captain called a halt. Taking Oscar to one side, he began to talk to him. Obviously he was trying a new approach. "Look, kid, if you'll just tell me where the guerrillas are, nothing will happen to you. I'll take you to my house and adopt you."

Oscar knew where the new base was, an alternative base planned for emergencies, but he did not know the whereabouts of his father. But nothing would persuade him to talk.

Then the captain, the same man who had ordered the death of up to 80 people, put his arm around Oscar and began to talk in a loving, considerate tone. "Listen. I know what you have been through. I'm guilty of destroying your family. You won't understand, but we are in a war with rebels. I was under orders to do that. I didn't want to. If you will just give me something to tell the colonel so I don't have to turn you over to him, I'll protect you. I don't want to take you to headquarters."

This was much harder for Oscar to handle than the threats. He was only a little boy, who was now an orphan. He had been strong for so long. After all he'd been through he needed some kind words, some understanding. He began to think that maybe the captain was sincere. Looking off toward the hills, he was silent, and the captain waited breathlessly.

But then the whole horrible scene of the massacre swept over him again, and he remembered the training he had received. "Never, even under the threat of death, reveal anything." He looked the captain straight in the eye and shook his head.

Finally realizing that nothing was going to persuade this boy to turn traitor, the captain thought a few moments, then said, "I'll have to turn you over to the colonel, but I'll help you all I can. They will interrogate you, and I don't know what else, but I'll do what I can to help you."

With that, he gave the order to proceed to the base.

Chapter 11

*T*he captain and his troop marched to the military base, which was located on the outskirts of the same village where Oscar had lived in his grandmother's house. He was their prisoner. Though he knew where he was, he gave no sign of recognition. He was determined to give no information of any kind. *My family are all dead, anyway,* he thought.

It was ironic that it took a whole platoon to bring in a little boy, and the captain expected a volley of expletives when the colonel got his report. Oscar stood in front of them, facing the stern, red-faced, older commander. He'd been through so much that he didn't think there was any more they could do to him. But he was to learn that there is no limit to the depravity of cruel men.

The troops were dismissed, but the captain stayed to give his report. "We did find most of the Gomez family," he began, "but Manuel himself was not with them. All of his brothers were there, and their families. We liquidated all of them. This is Manuel's boy. We kept him alive, as we were sure he could tell us of the whereabouts of his father and the rest of the band. We have done everything possible to get information from the boy, but he won't talk."

"What kind of a captain are you?" the colonel shouted. "You've spent two months on this mission, and you bring me a little kid and tell me you can't make him talk!" His volume increased, and the veins stood out on his forehead. "We'll see whether this little animal will talk or not!" he hissed.

For the next hour Oscar endured the verbal abuse of the angry colonel. Finally he ordered a soldier to hold a gun to the child's head. "Now talk, you little two-legged pig, or we'll kill you."

But he could have been shouting to a tree. There was no response from the boy. The only thing he would say was *"No sé."*

Exasperated, the colonel barked to a guard, "Take him to the cold room and we'll see if he'll talk or not."

The cold room was a cell with rock walls. The dried blood splattered on the walls gave mute evidence of its use. Oscar submitted quietly to his fate. He was placed against the wall with both hands put in handcuffs and fastened to chains that put him in a spread-eagle position. Periodically someone came to ask him if he was ready to talk. He just shook his head. Now and then someone brought the simple prison food to him and stuffed it in his mouth too fast for him to chew or swallow. His only thought was *If they're going to kill me, I wish they would hurry and do it. Why should I live?*

On the third day the colonel himself came to the cell. There Oscar hung, spread eagle against the wall. A boy.

A mere child. But a child who would not be broken. Again the abuse—threats and intimidation that would have forced a grown man to say anything for release—but "the little rebel," as he was beginning to be called, remained firm. In his heart he resolved that they could kill him, but he would not talk.

The officer was beside himself with fury. Not only was he desperate for information, but to have his authority challenged by a little stubborn kid was more than he could tolerate. "Tell us what you know or die!" he screamed.

Oscar turned his head toward the towering man. "I want to die. Why do I want to live? I don't know why you brought me here."

The officer stomped out, swearing, banging the door in his rage.

A soldier brought some food and stuffed a tortilla in his mouth, but he couldn't eat. "If you don't talk, you will die," the guard told him.

"Kill me!" was the little fellow's only response.

Later that day the colonel came back—a raging maniac. The disregard of his authority by this little kid had put him over the edge. Between all kinds of verbal abuse and name-calling he shouted, "We'll kill you right now!" Jerking his head toward the guards, he spit, "When I give the order you will kill this animal! When I count to three, shoot!"

He began to count, *"Uno, dos . . ."* Oscar shut his eyes. *"Tres!"* the colonel shouted. A shot rang out. But, to his anguish, Oscar knew he was still alive. The guard had shot the wall. The furious officer grabbed his neck and shook him, teasing his knife over Oscar's throat.

"I want to die!" Oscar cried out. "Why should I live without my family?"

"Animal!" the man bellowed. He drew his knife across the wall above the boy's head with so much force the sparks flew.

Turning to a guard, the colonel shouted, "Bring the captain that brought this animal here."

The captain flinched when he walked in and saw the little boy held by chains, stretched out against the wall. Oscar was pale and drawn, and he could only imagine what the child had endured.

"Nothing but death is good enough for this insect," the colonel snarled. "It makes me furious to see him. He deserves to die! Take care of him!"

The captain turned from the eyes of the shackled boy and faced his superior, determination etching his face. He waited moments before speaking. Then drawing himself up even straighter, he faced his commander. "Sir, this is enough. I have obeyed your orders to the letter. Now you will obey me." He looked into the colonel's astonished eyes without flinching. Then turning to the four guards, he said, "Leave. Leave me with the colonel."

Alone with the officer, the captain began, "This is a child, now an orphan as the result of your order to kill his family. Now you are not going to kill him! You will kill me first, and if you kill us both, my brothers will kill you."

"How would I kill you, my best captain, for this animal?" the colonel sneered. Without another word, he turned heel and went out, slamming the metal door so hard the sparks flew.

Oscar watched in amazement as the captain sat down on a nearby bench, put his head down into his hands, and began to weep.

When he gained control, the captain began to talk. Only he and Oscar were in the cell. "I know that because you have been faithful to your values you are here. You are a child. You shouldn't be here. You are an innocent child, not responsible for any of this. You are an upright child, faithful to what you have been taught. This is the quality of men that our country needs. I am ashamed and plead your forgiveness for what I did to your family, even though I did it under orders. I have never seen a boy like you before."

Oscar listened to the man with wonder, tears flowing from his own eyes.

The captain went on, "I don't know what kind of a man you will become, but I am sure you will make your mark. I can't undo what I have done, but I want to give you something to remember me by. Although I killed your family, I am determined to save your life. All the records of your family were destroyed in the fire in your village, but I want to give you a new name. I want to give you my name. It is Salvador [Savior]. From now on your name will be Salvador. Since your life has been spared, I hope that someday you can save someone else's life too, and I hope you will remember that in spite of what I did to your family, that in the end I saved your life. Please forgive me!"

He slumped even lower on the bench, sobbing.

Soon the captain gently removed Oscar's handcuffs and chains and set him free. Then he embraced the astonished boy and told him, "I will be your protector as long as you are here. You don't need to be afraid anymore. Do you think you can trust me?" Oscar looked at the captain and slowly nodded. He hardly knew what to think or how to respond.

"First of all, we need to go and buy you some clothes." The captain took Oscar to his jeep and told him to climb in. The boy had been through so much—even at the hands of this same man—that he couldn't believe the change in his attitude. He was suspicious. The man seemed sincere, but an apology and tears do not wipe out murder and torture.

Solemnly, Oscar sat beside the captain, and they rode to the general store. His clothes were ragged and dirty. He was weak from lack of proper food and cruel treatment. And emotionally, he felt dead. At the general store Oscar was outfitted with better clothes than he'd seen since leaving his home years before. Captain Salvador even bought him some toys appropriate for his age. It seemed he couldn't do enough. Cautious, suspicious, wondering what was going to happen next—Oscar's former training helped him to receive the gifts and gestures of friendship with courtesy.

The captain knew that Oscar needed nourishing food, so after leaving the store he suggested, "Let's go and get something to eat." They walked across the street to a small cafe. The hot soup was a good beginning, and then there was a plate of beans and rice with tortillas. Oscar couldn't eat a lot, but a good meal was what he needed. The whole time he ate, the captain talked to him, assuring him that he'd receive good care at the base. "I'll make arrangements for you to stay in the barracks with the soldiers, and they are going to know that you are the bravest little soldier I've ever seen. Don't worry; you won't have to deal with that colonel anymore!"

Leaving the café, the captain turned to Oscar. "First of all, we're going to make out new documents for you. Let's head over to that building across the street." He took him to the municipal office, just one room with a young man at a desk. "We need to apply for a new birth certificate for this boy. His papers were lost in a fire."

They sat on a nearby bench while the papers were drawn up. When the clerk finally handed the documents to the captain, man and boy walked out to the jeep. Before starting the engine, Captain Salvador turned to Oscar and handed him the documents. "Here are your papers, Oscar. You now have a new birth certificate, and your name is Salvador Gomez." He paused and looked at him tenderly. "Please remember me as your friend."

Chapter (12)

As Captain Salvador steered the army jeep down the dusty road to the base, he talked to Oscar, trying to assure him that he was no longer in danger.

"I doubt if you ever even see the colonel again, Oscar." He still used the boy's real name, knowing that it would be the boy's own choice if he ever used the name Salvador. "Just remember that some of these soldiers were with us on the march in the mountains. Most of them probably have little brothers, and it wasn't their idea to do what they did to your family or to you. They can't help admiring a boy with the stamina of a man. You don't need to be afraid anymore."

Oscar wanted to believe him, but he was still filled with terrible, conflicting emotions. The captain did seem sincere, he reasoned, especially back there in the cell when he broke down sobbing for what he had done. And since then, his kindness was a complete turnaround. But Oscar still felt a numbness, as though he were caught in a terrible nightmare. Surely he would wake up soon and find it was all a horrible dream.

When they parked in front of the barracks, the captain jumped out, saying, "Come on, Oscar. We're going to find you a place to stay."

The captain arranged for a bed in the barracks for Oscar. At first the boy was afraid to stay there. He knew the colonel resented his presence, but strangely, his few encounters with the superior were uneventful. The man simply ignored him. However, the change in the captain's attitude proved sincere. No one ever questioned Oscar again.

Soon after being installed in the barracks, he was at the mess hall during an evening meal. He recognized one of the soldiers at his table as one of the guards on the long difficult march in the mountains. *He even had part in the murder of my family,* he thought as a stab of pain seized him in the pit of his stomach. Overwhelming emotions of anger, grief, and desperation filled his mind.

He looked at the young soldier, fighting the ever-present surge of fear and hate. To his surprise, the soldier spoke to him. "How's it going, Oscar? Are they treating you better now?"

Oscar only nodded, but the soldier continued, "You know, fella, I've never seen a kid like you. I could never have stood up to the pressure like you did. A lot of us wished we could have helped you, but you know how it is in the army. You just take orders. Even the captain is really a decent guy. He was under orders, too. This whole business of this civil war is a mess. If there is anything you need, just let me know."

Oscar began to notice that other soldiers treated him

kindly too. The next evening, just before reveille, the soldier on the next bunk spoke to him. "Were you really with the rebels?"

Oscar stiffened. Adrenaline shot through him. *Are they still trying to get me to talk?* But then the soldier continued, "Never mind. It's nobody's business. I heard you were the bravest, toughest little kid this army has ever seen. The captain told some of us he wished there were more kids like you in the world, kids that stand up for what they believe."

Every day that went by, Oscar felt more accepted and safe. He knew that his new friend, the captain, was responsible for the way he was being treated. Another of the soldiers—a man from the captain's platoon on the day of the massacre—cornered him one day on the ball field. "I've been wanting to tell you, Oscar, that I feel for you. Even if they treat you good now, I know you'll never get over what they did to your family. I couldn't stand to see it. I've got a mother, father, and brothers and sisters. I kept thinking, *What if it were my family, what would I do?* I have a little brother about your age. I miss him a lot, and I can't stand to think what he would do and how he would feel if he had been in your place."

The pain of the weeks was still so sharp in his heart and the horrible picture still so vivid in his mind that Oscar could not talk about it. Although he appreciated the sympathy and understanding, whenever it was brought up, tears rushed to his eyes, and he could not speak.

Seeing his tortured look, the soldier went on, "As young men, it is our duty to serve our time in the army, but I don't believe in war. I hate what is happening in our country. I don't blame the military leaders alto-gether. They think they are defending the country, but war brings out the worst in people."

Nights were the worst for Oscar. Nightmares were a constant occurrence. He would wake up in a sweat, re-living the past weeks, then hoping that it was all a bad dream, and finally facing the reality that it was not. Then sometimes his dreams took him back to the happy days on his parents' farm when he followed his father around, herding the cattle, walking over the green fields, feeling the peace and security of his childhood. He'd awake in a cold sweat to the hard reality of being in the army barracks among strangers. Then, reliving the tortures of the past weeks, he would bury his head and soak his pillow with hidden tears.

He knew he would never see his brothers, sisters, or mother again, but where was his father? Was he dead too? How he longed to know if his father lived. He knew his father could never come near the barracks even if he were alive. He was a hunted man, and would surely be killed if found.

Captain Salvador was concerned for Oscar. He lived with his wife and children in the nearby military hous-ing complex. He could not bring himself to reveal the whole truth of the massacre to his wife, but he told her enough of the story to show the bravery of the little boy at the barracks, and how he had stood up to the colonel for Oscar. One Sunday when they were planning an outing for the children, she suggested, "Why don't you ask Oscar to go with us? He needs to be around some other children."

"That's a great idea," the captain agreed. "I'm sure he'd like that."

The following Sunday Oscar piled into the back of the jeep with the captain's children. For a few hours he almost forgot his sorrow. The boys flew kites with the help of Captain Salvador, and splashed in the nearby stream during the hottest part of the day. When the captain's wife called that dinner was ready, Oscar ate the home-cooked food with gusto. It was the typical beans, tortillas, and rice, but not cooked military style. The tortillas were hot and soft. The fried chicken and different fruits were a special treat. The day didn't last long enough for Oscar, but he slept better that night in his bunk at the barracks than he had for a long time.

Although Oscar gradually lost most of his fear and distrust of those around him, he was anxious about the future. What would happen next? The captain had explained that he would stay at the barracks until a better place was found for him. In one sense he feared leaving Captain Salvador, the only person he thought he could trust. But being among the soldiers was a constant reminder of the tragedy he had suffered. During the day different activities diverted his mind, and the captain had not forgotten him. But he dreaded the nights, alone with his thoughts in the dark. In an effort to obliterate the scene of his family's slaughter, and the pools of blood—especially the deep-red pools of blood—he'd struggle to remember some of the happy times of his childhood. On one such occasion, a vivid picture filled his mind. It was the evening he had walked out to the yard in front of their house at the farm. He'd stopped as he heard some beautiful music, the most beautiful his little boy's ears remembered hearing. Going a little farther, he saw his parents sitting on the trunk of the fallen tree, arm in arm, facing the setting sun, and singing that song. After that he remembered hearing his mother sing that same song as she worked in her kitchen and as she scrubbed their clothes on a rock at the river, *"Oh, Señor, Siempre escucha mi canto, Para siempre contigo estaré."* ("Oh, Lord, forever hear my song, forever to be with Thee!") The memory of his mother in the home that had held only security and love for him would mesh with the horror of the massacre. He hadn't seen it, of course, but he could picture a soldier slicing a machete across his mother's throat. Remembering his last glimpse of his sister as they dragged her away plunged him again in unbearable agony and grief. Over and over the two pictures invaded his mind—his mother, his sister—especially during the long night hours when he suffered alone in the dark, soaking his pillow with tears.

The captain stopped to see Oscar almost every day. If he was going anywhere in his jeep he'd take the boy along, and slowly the friendship between them grew. At first Oscar could not harmonize the captain's friendly attitude with the vivid mental picture of the captain giving orders to kill his family. However, his need for a friend was great, and the captain had shown regret and guilt for what he'd had to do. With the simplicity of a child, Oscar reasoned, "He had to do it. He didn't want to, and he is sorry." Gradually, Captain Salvador found a place in the heart of the little boy he had so greatly wronged.

Chapter 13

*O*scar was sitting on a bench in front of the military office one morning when Captain Salvador drove up in his jeep. "Come here, Oscar," he called. "I want to talk to you."

Oscar sat down in the passenger's seat and listened as the captain began to explain the plan he had for him. "You know, this really isn't a place for children to live. We've been in contact with General García, the head of our country's armed forces. He's been involved in the civil war in this area. Many other children besides you have lost their parents, too, and General García has a special interest in looking out for orphaned kids. He knows about you, too. He'll be here this next week, and he'll probably have an idea of a better place for you to live."

Oscar's heart beat faster. Noticing the stricken look in the boy's eyes, Captain Salvador tried to assure him. "After all that's happened to you, I wouldn't blame you for being afraid to go to some new place. But don't worry. I feel sure you can trust General García. He has the reputation of liking children and trying to help them."

"Will he take me far away from here?" the boy asked.

"I don't know, Oscar, but I'll try to talk to him and explain your situation. I'm sure he is thinking of finding you a home where you can go to school."

Oscar waited with anticipation as well as anxiety for the general's visit. It was boring to hang around the barracks with no other boys his age to be with, and he wanted to go to school. But the unknown was scary.

One morning he heard people running. "The general's helicopter is landing right out in the ball field!" one of the soldiers told him.

Oscar followed the others out to meet him. It was a beautiful white helicopter. The general stepped out, dressed in his crisp uniform. The brass and medals on his coat were impressive. The soldiers stood in awe, but the general's big smile put them at ease. Almost immediately the little boy caught his eye. Walking over toward him, the general asked, "Is this Oscar?"

Oscar smiled timidly, but extended his hand. *"Oscar Gómez, a sus órdenes, señor."* ("Oscar Gomez, at your orders, sir.")

Later that day a messenger found Oscar and told him that the general was waiting in the office to talk to him. Oscar hurried to obey. He'd never talked to a general before, but more than that, he knew that this visit would affect his future. There was anxiety in his eyes as he entered the office.

"Well, Oscar, I'm glad to see you. I've been hearing about this brave boy here." Standing up from behind the desk, the general walked over to a bench. "Sit down here beside me and let's talk." His tone was friendly and disarming, and almost immediately Oscar felt comfortable with him. Maybe he could trust him, as Captain Salvador had said he could.

"I know some of what has happened to you, Oscar, and I am sorry. There are a lot of things that you probably don't know or wouldn't understand, but this war is bad, and I know it has done something terrible to you. I can't change what has happened, but I am here to try to help you. We need to find a place where you can live and go to school. For right now, I want to take you to the military hospital in the capital. Other children are there who have lost their parents too. We want to see if you need any medical attention. I see you have a bandage on your arm. What happened?"

"I was running and a soldier shot at me," Oscar said simply.

"Well, you can tell me more about that later," the general replied. "You can get your things together and be ready to leave with me tomorrow morning. OK?"

"Sí, señor," the boy answered respectfully. Then he couldn't resist asking, "Sir, will we be going in your helicopter?"

"Right. Is that OK with you?" the general asked with a smile.

With his eyes big with excitement, Oscar quickly replied, "Yes, sir!"

Later that day Captain Salvador came by. "So you're going to the capital?"

"I guess so," Oscar said. He wasn't sure if he was glad or not, especially to leave the captain. But then he brightened. "I'm going to ride in the general's helicopter," he said.

"Well, now, that really is something. I've never had a chance to do that."

"Do you know how long I'll be at the military hospital? What will happen next?"

"No, I haven't talked to the general, but I've heard that he really looks after kids like you who've lost their homes and parents. I'm sure he wants to take you to where you can go to school." The captain looked fondly at the little boy. "Why don't we go for one last ride, Oscar? Maybe you'd like to go out to my place and tell my kids goodbye. They're always asking about you."

"I would like that, sir. You've been kind to me."

For the next hour Oscar played ball with the captain's son, and serious thoughts were put aside. When it was time to go, he said goodbye to the family who had befriended him. He knew they were the one good thing he would remember about his days at the military base.

Back at the barracks, Captain Salvador reached over and gave Oscar a hug. "I'll never forget you, my boy. Someday I hope you'll remember me as a friend who respects and admires you for what you are." It was all he could say as tears filled his eyes. He knew—and wished he could forget—that Oscar would also have to remember him for the worst day of his life.

They shook hands like men, and the boy looked him straight in the eye. "I won't forget you, Captain. You saved my life, and I will remember that you have given me your name." As the captain backed away, Oscar gave a last wave, and then stood watching the jeep go down the road.

The next morning a little boy sat behind the pilot,

and the general sat in the copilot's seat. When the big white bird lifted into the air, Oscar thrilled with excitement. He never dreamed that he would ride in a helicopter. He felt a wave of sadness as he left the hills and valleys that had always been his home, and there was some fear in sailing off into the unknown. But the past month had taught him that everyone wasn't mean, and this general seemed like someone he could trust.

Chapter 14

*T*he helicopter lifted high into the air as the general spoke to the pilot. "Keep her up. You never know when some of these rebels might be in the hills and try to take a shot at us." They were flying over mountains, hills, and valleys far from any city or heavily populated area. But looking out the window, Oscar could see a village now and then. Toward the north were the mountains where he and his family had been in hiding with the guerrilla army. *Is my father down there someplace,* he wondered.

Hiding places were plentiful, and the peasants living there were vulnerable to the misleading tactics of the guerrillas.

Sighting another village in the distance, the general directed, "Let's take a look down here. There was a recent skirmish, but the army is in control now." Slowly they descended, hovering low enough to assess the situation.

The scene below them was of utter devastation. Much of the village had been burned, and the rest seemed to be deserted. Taking several turns, they passed over what looked like a garbage dump. "Wait a minute!" the general said. "Look over there! I see something moving. It could be a child. I thought this village was abandoned! Let's take a look." And the big bird settled down in a nearby field.

The general jumped to the ground, heading for the area where they'd seen movement. To his shock, he found a small girl. She was in her native dress, a wraparound, hand-woven skirt, and brightly colored hand-woven blouse. Her long hair had been braided, but it was disheveled. Her face was smudged with dirt and smeared with her tears. She backed away from him, fear in her eyes.

"What is your name, little girl?" the general asked kindly as he bent down to her level.

She wouldn't answer, just looked at him, shrinking back. "Well, we can't leave her here alone," he told himself. "She's another victim of this blasted war! I may be a general, but I hate what this war does to the children. It isn't their fault!"

He led the little girl over to the helicopter, and she went somewhat reluctantly. When he lifted her up to the open door, he told the pilot, "Here's another one of these children. Who knows who she is? Her parents are probably dead."

The little girl huddled beside the window on the other side of Oscar. He knew how she must feel, and he tried to smile at her to give her some assurance.

The helicopter began to descend as they neared the capital city, landing at one end of the international airport in front of the army headquarters. As the rotor blades came to a stop, some soldiers rushed out to meet them, standing at attention as the general stepped down. "Send for my car," he ordered.

Soon a long, black, bulletproof limousine pulled up, and another soldier jumped out and stood at attention. *"A sus órdenes, mi general!"* he said. ("At your orders, my general!")

"Take us to the military hospital," the general told his chauffeur. Knowing the apprehension of the little girl, Oscar took her hand and talked to her in the dialect of the area. "Don't be afraid. This officer is trying to help us." The two wide-eyed children looked out the window as the big car rolled through the streets. Soon a gate was opened, and they drove onto the hospital grounds. An officer—who was the administrator—met them.

"I've brought two children from the conflict area, some more orphans, I suspect," the general said. "Have someone take them to the children's ward. I imagine they're hungry, but they need to be examined to see if they need any treatment."

"First of all, we need to know their names so we can make a record," the officer told them. "Once in a while some relative comes looking for a child."

The little girl still would not talk. When Oscar was asked his name, he thought for a moment, remembering the captain who had saved his life and befriended him. *The records of your family were lost in the fire in your village. I want to give you something to remember me by. My name is Salvador. From now on, that will be your name.* The captain had recorded his name on the military record books as Salvador. His family was gone. He might never see his village again, and he didn't want anyone to know that he'd been in a guerrilla camp. He wanted to forget it all for now.

He took a deep breath. "My name is Salvador Gómez."

Soon a kindly woman in white came and led the two children off to another part of the hospital. Salvador had lost most of his apprehension by then. This general really had a way with children, and he felt safe. The little girl was taken to a different ward for smaller children.

The next day when he went to an area where children were playing he could hardly believe his eyes. He looked at one of the little boys, and looked again. It was his cousin, Gaspar! And he'd thought all his family were dead.

"How did you get here?" he asked, amazed.

"When they started rounding up people, I ran away. Later when I went back to your house, I found it was empty, and someone told me they were all dead. When the soldiers went through the village they found me and brought me here."

"You're lucky that you ran away," Salvador told his cousin.

"What happened to you?" Gaspar asked.

Salvador's face grew dark with the memory. "It's a long story," he murmured. "I don't want to talk about it now, but I will tell you one thing. You are an orphan, and my mother is dead. I don't know about my father."

Gaspar turned away. What he'd feared most was true.

Salvador soon fell into the hospital routine. There were other boys to play with—some older, some younger. Some were sons of soldiers, there in the hospital for treatment. A few were orphans whose parents had died in one of the battles with the guerrillas.

Although they were well treated and had good food, a hospital was not a good place to live. Salvador was almost glad when the general came and told him that he'd found a home for him.

"It's a place out in the country where some good people have a home for orphan children," he said. "It isn't like some orphanages. You live in a house with house parents and other children. They have a school too." The boy's eyes brightened at that. During the three years at the guerrilla camp, there'd been no time to think of a school. His only schooling had been training camps to learn how to fight the army. "Tomorrow I'll take you there."

"Can Gaspar go there too?"

"Yes, several children will be going. Even that little girl who came into town with us."

The next morning when Salvador and Gaspar were taken to the big black car again, two other boys and the little girl climbed in too. Then a nurse came carrying a small child who was obviously sick. Oscar was seated in the car jump seat, and he turned to look at the child in the nurse's arms. She looked strangely familiar. Could it be his cousin, Ana? It had been more than a year since the tragedy that took away his family. Ana's parents were with them in the rebel camp. Their mothers were cousins and were close. This little girl was sick, too sick to talk. His mind went back to the day of the massacre. *I can't be sure, but I think it's Ana. If it is, I wonder how she escaped being killed. Her parents must have been in the line.* But he didn't discuss this discovery with anyone, not even Gaspar. Gaspar was a cousin from his father's side of the family and wouldn't remember Ana.

"This little girl should stay here at the hospital," the nurse told the general. "She's much too sick to leave."

"That's probably true," he agreed. "She was brought in only yesterday. But I can't make another trip out there right away. Those people will take good care of her, and there's a hospital wing out there at the base near the orphanage."

The nurse went along to help with the little girls, and a soldier came to guard the general. The black limousine with its strange cargo in the two rear seats and the general and his driver in front headed for the airport.

The boys' faces lit up when they saw that they'd be riding in the big white helicopter again. By now they felt more or less resigned to whatever future awaited them. But before boosting the children into the aircraft, the general stood before them. "I'm taking you to a beautiful place in the trees where some Christian people have made homes for children like you. Each of you will have a home with a father and mother and other children who will be like your brothers and sisters. There's a school there too. You can grow up there and feel like you belong in a family. I go to visit sometimes, so I'll see you once in a while." The girls were too small to understand, but Salvador and the others listened carefully. This general and the hospital staff had treated them kindly. They were beginning to lose their fear.

Soon they were all aboard and belted in. The huge blades began to turn, and slowly the big bird lifted into the air. It seemed that they were just above the tall buildings as they flew over the city. Then they turned north. Leaving civilization behind, they gained more altitude to scale the mountain ranges surrounding the city. After an hour's flight the land leveled out except for small mounds or little hills dotting the landscape. Then the military airport came into view, then the base, and finally a group of houses and buildings with an empty field, where the pilot lowered his craft.

When the rotor blades stopped, the general jumped out and began to unload the children. One of the orphanage house fathers ran up to see what was going on. He was speechless to see the general personally lifting children out of the craft.

"Can I help you?" the man offered.

"Just tell Mrs. Fleck I brought her some more children," the general replied as the pilot handed him the sick little girl. The general placed her in the house father's arms. "They found this little one in a cave. The mother must have hid her there and then did not make it back." Placing the other little girl on the ground, the general explained, "This one was left alone at a garbage dump." In just a few moments he was back in the helicopter, the engine revved up, and the dust flew as the blades began to whirl. With some trepidation Salvador watched the big bird soar off beyond the trees. There was nothing to do but follow the house father toward the homes.

Chapter 15

*F*rom the open field where the helicopter landed, Guillermo led the group of children, carrying the little sick one in his arms. Juana, the director, had heard the helicopter, and now she stood on the front porch and waited for them. When she saw them coming she hurried to meet them. "What happened?" she asked the man. "Was that the general bringing these children?"

"Yes; he seemed to be in a hurry. He just unloaded them, said they came from a battle area and that they are orphans. He said to tell Mrs. Fleck he brought her some children."

"Didn't he tell you anything more than that?"

"Well, he did say that the smallest girl was found in a cave and the other one at a garbage dump. This little one is really sick. Her mother must have hidden her and then was killed. Lucky for her that a soldier happened to find her," Guillermo added. "The general said that they came from the area of conflict in the high country."

Juana took the baby in her arms and looked at her closely. "She's so thin and pale and listless. I hope it isn't too late. Poor baby! Who knows what she's gone through. Help me get the children into the house, and then go and get your wife," she told Guillermo. "I'll need some help. We need to figure out where to put all these children."

In a few minutes Marina, Guillermo's wife, arrived. Juana could always count on her, and she could trust her with the smallest, most delicate babies. "We have a very sick little girl here, Marina. I need your help. For now, I want you to take care of the two girls. But first we must get the little one to the doctor. Please send someone for Job and tell him we need to go to the base hospital right away. Then please take the other children to your house until I get back and decide where to put them all."

In a few minutes Job, the plant administrator, arrived with the Toyota pickup, and Juana climbed in, the sick baby in her arms. "So the general brought us more children?" Job queried. "I heard a helicopter and wondered who it was."

"You know, ever since this civil war started, nearly every child we get is a victim of that violence. Sometimes both parents have been killed, but many times it is the husband who's killed and the wife can no longer support and care for her children," Juana observed. "I wonder how long it's going to last."

"The news we get by radio doesn't sound good. Right now the problem seems to be in the western highlands, but it's spreading. The revolutionaries are bent on destroying the army and the government."

Kindhearted Americans had started the orphanage

on part of the land owned by a mission school and called it "El Bosque" (The Forest), because of its dense trees. The military base, located nearby, was the main security for the northern section of the country. General García had been the commander at the base, but when the civil war escalated, he was moved to the capital, and promoted to be the head of the country's armed forces. While commanding the base, he often visited the mission school and the orphanage. Many times in his responsibilities, he found orphaned children and brought them to Juana. Even though he was a tough military man, he seemed to have a natural affinity for children. His visits were frequent enough that the children knew him and loved to have him come. Since being moved to the capital, he didn't come as often, but it was obvious he'd not forgotten the place that he considered a haven for homeless children.

They drove to the base hospital unit and were soon ushered into the doctor's waiting room. When the secretary learned that General García himself had brought this child in his helicopter he quickly led them into an examining room.

"So you have a little war victim here," the doctor said, gently beginning his examination. "Do you know anything about her?"

"Doctor, we don't even know her name or how old she is. The general said that she was found by a soldier in a cave, evidently left there by a mother who couldn't come back for her. She cries and puts her hand to her ear, and you can see it's badly infected. I'm sure she was without food or water for some time."

The doctor examined her ear first. "From the smell and the look of it, I'm afraid gangrene has set in," he said grimly. "Obviously, she's malnourished and dehydrated too. We'll get some specimens for the lab first of all." The doctor's serious, businesslike manner showed his concern. But he handled the child with such gentleness and earnestness that Juana knew the little girl would get the very best that this doctor and this hospital had to offer.

"We'd better keep her here until she stabilizes," the doctor told Juana as he finished the examination. "We have to watch that ear. It looks like an insect bite that became infected. We need to watch her electrolytes too. She's very dehydrated. You can stay here with her if you like, or come back in the morning to see how she is."

Juana was hesitant to leave, but she needed to go back and arrange for the care of the other new children. "Doctor, I must go back to El Bosque. The general brought five other children and they need my attention. But I'll come back later tonight and stay with the baby."

"Fine," the doctor replied. "You can come with us to see her into her room. We'll watch her closely."

The nurses had already started intravenous fluids when Juana looked again at the small form under the white sheet. Silently she prayed, "Dear Father, this is one of Your little children. Please send an angel to stay here with her, and please don't let her die. All she needs is Your healing touch."

As Juana and Job drove back through the night to El Bosque, Job was anxious to know what the doctor said.

"He said that she's a very sick little girl, but I can tell

that he's doing everything he can for her. He is a good doctor. I'm so thankful to have good medical care so far out here in the jungle."

"One thing the army does is to provide the best medical care for their soldiers. They always send good doctors and staff to their hospitals," Job commented.

Then Juana began thinking of the other children waiting back at El Bosque. *The other little girl didn't seem sick, but she was thin and small. I wonder how old she is.* Her thoughts jumped to the four boys. *They seem well enough. Of course they're all somewhat frightened, not knowing what to expect, and being victims of the war. They have lost their parents. They might tell us what happened, but they might not. Some things are just too painful to talk about.*

Driving up to her home, she found that Marina had taken the other five children to her house. She and Guillermo served as parents in one of the cottages. The plan at El Bosque was to create families of parents and children so the children wouldn't feel like orphans anymore. These young victims needed more than food and a roof over their heads. They needed the warmth of family, of a daddy and mommy, of love and security.

Juana walked over to the house, the first one built when El Bosque was founded. Marina was making the children feel at home and had asked the other children to bring out some toys. But Juana knew that they couldn't all stay at Marina's. She already had eight children, and 12 was considered maximum. The two older boys would find room in House Two with José and his wife.

After learning their names, she thought, *This younger boy has a lot of pain in his eyes, and fear too. Since Gaspar is his cousin, they should stay together. I think I would rather leave them here with Marina and Guillermo. And, for now, we'll leave the little girl here too.* Turning to the small girl, she noticed fear in her large, dark, expressive eyes. Children were always afraid when they first came. "What is your name, dear?" she asked, bending down to the level of the child.

"Rosita," the child answered timidly. But when Juana tried to get her to say more, she refused. She was dressed in the typical, handwoven dress of the highlands people. When Juana and Marina gave her some new, clean clothing, she refused to change. She didn't want those Western-style clothes. She clung to her little typical skirt and blouse and insisted on wearing them.

"Well, let her wear them until she is ready to change," Juana advised Marina.

Juana turned to the younger boy. "What did you say your name is, son?" she asked as she sat on the sofa and pulled the little fellow over beside her.

"My name is Salvador, ma'am," he answered respectfully. She was struck by a certain look in his eyes. It was an intense, pained expression. He seemed withdrawn and shy, but she was accustomed to receiving new children, and most of them came from tragic backgrounds. Still, the look in this boy's eyes drew her to him. *What terrible secret or burden is he carrying in his heart?* she wondered. *All of these children have been orphaned, but there is something deeper here.* She knew that this was not the time to probe. Right now he needed assurance and love. And Juana had plenty of that.

Then she turned to the cousin. "And what is your name?"

"I am Gaspar. We are cousins, but we really like to be brothers, especially since," and he dropped his eyes, "since our parents were killed."

"Very well, you can be brothers and stay together. For now you will stay with Mami Marina and Papi Guillermo [pronounced Mommy and Poppy]. Shall we go and see your room?" Juana and Marina took the boys into one of the four bedrooms and led them to a set of bunk beds.

"Who wants to sleep on top?" Marina asked with a smile.

"I will. I'm older," Gaspar answered.

Before Juana left, the supper table was being set—a long table made of a four- by eight-foot sheet of plywood, covered with Formica. Long benches sat on either side for the children, and a chair was at each end for the parents.

"I hope everything goes well here tonight," Juana told Marina as she went to the door. She smiled her confidence that Marina knew how to make children feel loved and at home. "I've got to go back to the hospital and see how the baby is doing."

It was dark as she went along the path to her home. "You never know what a day will bring," Juana murmured. "I must get word to Mami Fleck about these new children." Six new children all at once. She felt thankful for International Children's Care. Begun just four years before, no one could have imagined that a civil war in their country would bring so many war orphans to the homes."

Chapter 16

Supper was announced soon after Juana left. Guillermo, the house father, had come in from his work. "I'm glad we have some new members in our family," he remarked with a smile.

"Yes," Marina replied, adding for the benefit of the rest of the children, "they came in a helicopter today. General García brought them" She stooped, then lifted up the little girl. And this is Rosita."

"Welcome, Rosita," the jovial man greeted her. Guillermo was about six feet tall and must have seemed awesome to the children.

"And this is Salvador and Gaspar. They are cousins." Their new father put out his hand to shake with each of them, then gave them each a big hug. "We are so glad you have come to be part of our family, boys. And since we're all a family here, from now on I will call you my sons, and Rosita, I will call you my daughter. If you want to, you can call me Papi."

"Let's all gather around the table," Marina called. "Rosita, you can sit here on the end of the bench near me. Salvador, why don't you sit on the other end near

Papi, and Gaspar, you can sit right across from him on the other side of Papi."

When everyone was seated, Guillermo announced, "Here at our house we always fold our hands, bow our heads, close our eyes, and pray to God in heaven to thank Him for the food He has given us, and to ask Him to bless it to our health. Let's all bow our heads."

Salvador had never seen anyone pray before eating and he felt strange, but all the other children quickly obeyed. He glanced around, and all their eyes were shut and their heads bowed. He followed their example.

There was no electricity at El Bosque except when the generator was turned on, but candles cast a soft, pleasant glow around the room. The house was a simple, rectangular design—four bedrooms, one at each corner, with a large open living area in the middle. The kitchen was at the back of the open space, and the living room at the front, with the large table dividing the two areas. A bathroom at each end of the house separated the two bedrooms. A covered back porch provided a place to wash clothes.

Sitting at the table by candlelight suddenly brought back memories to Salvador of his childhood back on the farm. It was the first time he'd sat at a table, family style, since leaving his home for the training camp. In one sense, it felt good to be in a family atmosphere again, but the memories flooding his mind made him want to cry. "No, I won't cry here," he told himself. "No one would understand, and I can't talk about it."

When everyone finished eating, Mami Marina and some of the bigger children quickly cleared the table and washed the dishes. Salvador and Gaspar felt awkward, not knowing what to do. They just stood off to one side.

But Papi Guillermo knew how to make children feel at home. He went to the sofa by the front window and called, "Come, boys. Sit here by me. We need to get acquainted." Warily, the boys obeyed. The man arranged one boy on each side of him with an arm around each. "How old are you, Gaspar?"

"I am almost 12, sir," the boy answered.

"And you, Salvador?"

In a low voice he said, "I just had my tenth birthday."

"And what kinds of things do you like to do?" Guillermo was trying to draw them out. He couldn't know that their past several years had not been spent in child's play, but in men's games of violence and war. He couldn't know that their young minds had been brainwashed with a hate and fear of the army, the enemy.

But there had been some periods of play, too. "Well, we like to play soccer," Gaspar ventured.

"Great! We have a field near here where we play sometimes," the man told them. "Of course there's work to do too. Maybe you boys would like to go to the farm with me tomorrow. We're planting gardens." The boys both agreed. Salvador remembered working with his father in their garden and cornfield.

Before long the kitchen was cleaned. Mami Marina and the other children came to the living area and found places to sit. Some of the children sat on the floor. Rosita sat on Marina's lap.

"Here at El Bosque we have a beautiful custom,"

Guillermo explained to the newcomers. "We like to start and end our days in worshiping our Father in heaven. You know, He is the one who made this world, who made us, and who gives us all the good things we have in life. But first of all, we'll sing some songs."

The two new boys just sat there listening to all these strange new customs. Salvador, especially, enjoyed hearing them sing. They didn't need any songbooks, for everyone seemed to know all the words. After two or three songs, Guillermo told them a story from the Bible. "A long time ago there was a young boy, maybe about your age, Gaspar, whose father had a big ranch. The boy's name was David, and he learned to care for his father's sheep. Now David and his family knew and served the true God of heaven, and David had learned to pray to God and to believe that God heard and answered his prayers.

"One day when David was way out in the hills with the sheep, a lion came and tried to kill one of the sheep. David was frightened, but he thought right away about praying and asking God to help him. And do you know that David had so much faith that he went right over there and took a big stick and killed that lion and rescued the sheep? Another day the same thing happened with a bear. David was a brave boy, but he was brave because he knew he could trust God to help him."

Salvador listened, entranced, to the story. He could relate to David taking care of his father's sheep. He had helped his father with the cattle. But he had never before heard of praying when there is danger.

After the story they sang another song, and then

everyone knelt down. The boys hesitated, but seeing the rest with their heads bowed and their hands folded, they bowed their heads. But they did not close their eyes. Guillermo's prayer included the new children. "And Father, I ask that You bless these precious children who have come to us today. You know why they are here, and You can comfort their hearts. Help them to learn how much You love them."

When they all arose, Marina announced bedtime. "First of all, everyone brush your teeth and then put on your pajamas," she directed. She went to get Rosita ready for bed, and Guillermo took Salvador and Gaspar to show them where to put their things, and give them each a pair of pajamas. They were given toothbrushes too.

Finally, every child was bedded down and the candles blown out. Marina and Guillermo were in their bedroom talking over their day. "Every time they bring us a new child, I wonder how we can really make that child feel at home and secure," Marina said. "It must be frightening to suddenly find yourself with strangers and be told that they will be your parents. Who knows how they've been treated before. And they have no idea what will happen to them now."

"That is true," her husband said, "and chances are that many have been abused, neglected, hungry, or even abandoned by their parents. But according to General García, the children who came today were all victims of the war. You know that the terrorists go into the villages and cause friction between the people and the army. Sometimes innocent bystanders are caught in the crossfire." He paused, thoughtful. "I think these children have suffered more than most. I heard that the general said these children come from an area where all the adults died in a confrontation with the army. They must have been connected to the guerrillas, or at least the army thought so."

In the room where the two boys were placed, Salvador lay on the bottom bunk with his eyes wide open in the darkness. So many things had happened that day. So far, nothing bad had happened, but the experiences of his past three years made it difficult to trust people. Fear, suspicion, hate, and vengeance had been such a part of his life since losing his family that he found it hard to think that these new parents could truly be trustworthy. He didn't believe anyone could be trusted.

Then thoughts of his mother and father and his brothers and sisters started the tears flowing. The scene of the killings flooded his mind again, and he hid his head under the sheet sobbing quietly. Soon his pillow was wet. He would not cry out, but his heart cried in silence. *Oh! Why didn't I die too?*

At last he drifted into sleep, but with sleep came the terrible dreams. They were always the same—he was running, running, running from someone, reaching out for his mother. But he couldn't find her. He searched for his father, but he searched in vain.

Chapter 17

With the crowing of a rooster outside his window Salvador woke with a start. *Where am I?* he wondered. Looking up to the bunk above him he saw Gaspar still asleep. Then he remembered. This was his new home and the family was already astir, for he heard pans rattling in the kitchen, and someone was running water into the *pila* (washtub) on the back porch.

Before long, Papi Guillermo was at their door calling, *"Buenos Dias, hijos. Ya es tiempo de levantarse!"* ("Good morning, children. It is time to get up.") He gave both boys a towel and showed them how to use the shower when their turn came. There was no hot water, but in that tropical climate the water was only cool and the air was warm.

When all the children were up and dressed, the family gathered in the living room for morning worship. They started out with a song, "Lord, in the morning Thou shalt hear My voice ascending high; To Thee will I direct my prayer, To thee lift up mine eye." Salvador wasn't sure if he liked the idea of worship morning and night, but he did enjoy the singing. He listened to the words and tried to learn the tune. Papi Guillermo opened a black book that he called his Bible. "I am going to read a verse this morning, and I wonder how many of us can remember it today. I am reading from Psalm 46, the first verse. 'God is our refuge and strength, a very present help in trouble.' It is a short verse and will be easy to remember, but it is a very important verse. No matter where you are, or what kind of a problem you have, remember this verse." Then, going around the circle, he helped each child to repeat it.

Salvador listened carefully. Was it really true that God is a help in trouble? And who was God anyway? He had heard the word God before and had a vague idea of some supernatural being, but no one had ever really explained who God is or made Him seem real. Then the angry, tormenting thoughts took over. God couldn't be the loving person this new father talked about. If that were so, why had He let all his family be killed? And the bitterness rose up, nearly choking him. *That God didn't help me.* They sang another song, and Papi Guillermo asked one of the children to pray.

Soon everyone found their place at the long table. Faces were shining, and hair was still damp but combed and slicked down. All the children sat respectfully until Guillermo told them to bow their heads for the blessing. *There sure is a lot of praying in this house!* Salvador thought. The food was simple, but there was plenty of it. A huge bowl of hot oatmeal, milk, freshly squeezed orange juice, homemade bread, and a large platter of bananas made up the menu. No one complained of not being hungry, and everyone ate heartily.

When all the plates were empty, each one helped to

clear the table. Salvador and Gaspar followed the example of the other children. Then Marina announced that it was time to make beds. The older children ran to the bedrooms, and soon everything was in order. A young woman lived there to help Marina with the dishes, the cleaning, and washing the clothes. The smaller children went out in the yard to play, and the school-age children went to school.

Salvador was wondering what he and Gaspar were supposed to do when the director, Juana, came to the door. They soon learned that she was called Señorita Juana, or Seño' Juana for short.

"*Buenos dias,* Salvador and Gaspar. Did you sleep well last night?" she greeted them.

"*Si, seño,*" they answered respectfully. But Salvador knew it wasn't really the truth. He had slept fitfully with the same horrible dreams.

"I've come to take you to school," she announced. "Have you been to school before?"

Both boys shook their heads. Salvador and Gaspar had both taken lots of classes at the camp, but it was all in training to be guerrillas, to be part of the rebellion against the government.

She walked with them down the graveled road that wound around the circle through the pine trees. The children's houses were arranged among the trees, each one on an acreage on the outside of the circle that made the central campus. The school was at the far end of the circle.

The boys felt apprehensive, but Salvador had always wanted to go to school. He worried that he might be one of the biggest in the first grade, but he soon found that there were children of all ages in the first grade. He wasn't the only one who had not been in a school before. The teacher gave them each a desk, a pencil, and notebook. Salvador soon learned that school was an escape for him. He was learning new things, and there wasn't time to think much about his grief.

School started at 8:00 and let out by 12:30. Salvador found it a little hard at recess when the other children ran out to play. At first he just waited and watched, but soon the other boys took him into their ball game and he was one of them.

When the bell rang dismissing school, they went back along the road to their house where dinner was already on the table. Guillermo came in from working out on the farm, and soon everyone was washed and at their place. Salvador was hungry, and the food looked good. After the blessing, Marina spoke. "Salvador, you can help yourself to the beans there by you, and then pass them on." Besides the black beans and rice, he saw cooked carrots and sliced tomatoes. His mouth watered at the sight of a stack of hot, handmade tortillas in the middle of the table—tortillas made from corn ground that morning. Salvador knew already that this mother made good food, and he hadn't had good, home-cooked food for a long, long time.

After dinner Papi Guillermo announced that all the bigger boys could go to the farm with him. "Gaspar, you and Salvador can come too. There's plenty of weeding to do." When they'd all changed into their work clothes, Guillermo led his troop down the road, past all the homes, and on to the farm. New little bean shoots were just breaking through the ground. He explained how to tell the difference between bean plants and weeds, and the boys happily went to work.

Daily, each of the families at El Bosque followed the same general plan, and the boys soon got used to the routine. Salvador tried to cooperate at home and at school. He liked his new parents, but he didn't want to call them Mami and Papi yet, like the other children did. On the surface it seemed that he was adjusting well, but Juana noticed that he was always deeply sober and withdrawn. She knew he'd suffered a terrible loss and everything was very strange for him, but he didn't offer to tell her or his house parents anything about his past. In fact, he avoided the subject. Little did they know that inside he lived with devastating turmoil.

The days were busy and Salvador felt more and more at home, but in sleep the horrible nightmares continued. Hate and desire for vengeance on those who had killed his family was eating him up. Sometimes he felt that he must vent his anger on someone. In the darkness he suffered agonies as the horrible scene of the massacre came back into his mind. Many times he lay awake until after midnight, and when he slept he'd often jerk awake from the ever-present dreams. Sometimes he dreamed he was back on the farm, and those dreams were almost worse, for then he'd awake with the awful realization that that life was gone forever. Other times as he relived the horror of the massacre in his sleep, he'd awaken in a cold sweat. *Someday I will avenge the death of my family,* he often thought, believing that doing so would finally bring him relief.

Chapter (18)

*A*few days later the doctor told Juana that she could take the baby home. "It will take some time for her to completely recuperate, but she's out of danger," he asurred her. "Her ear is healing and the dysentery is under control. I'll give you a prescription."

Since Juana had spent so much time with her at the hospital, the little one went to her gladly. Juana dressed her with some of the pretty little clothes that had been sent in a shipment from the International Children's Care office in Vancouver, Washington. Job was driving the pickup again, and on the way back through the jungle they discussed this latest group of children.

Juana looked down at the child in her arms. "From what the general said, this little girl had a close brush with death. If a soldier hadn't happened to go into that cave where she'd been hidden, she wouldn't have lasted much longer. God must have something special in mind for her."

"I'm sure that is so," Job nodded. "I remember hearing Señora Fleck say that these orphaned children are special in God's eyes. Do you know her name?"

"No, we don't know anything about her—neither her name nor how old she is. We'll have to give her a name, and the doctor will have to help us decide about when she was born."

Arriving at El Bosque, Job stopped at the gate in front of Juana's house. The girl that helped her came running out. "Oh! You brought the baby home! Is she all right now?"

"Well, she is better, but it will be a while before she's really well," Juana answered. Then she directed the girl, "Please go and tell Marina in House One and Ellie in House Four to come. And tell Marina to bring Rosita." The girl ran off down the road leading to the children's homes. Each house stood on approximately five acres. Houses were separated by a field and trees.

When both house mothers arrived, Juana invited them into her little parlor. She'd placed the baby, now asleep, on her bed. "Marina has been taking care of Rosita temporarily, but her house is really full, and she has two of the boys. I would like you, Ellie, to take the two little girls. I think it would be nice to keep them together. They aren't related, but they did come from the same area of the country." Then turning to Marina, she asked, "How is Rosita doing?"

"She's doing fine. She seems contented, though she doesn't talk yet. I think she must have come from an area where they speak one of the dialects. But no one is going to take away that little typical outfit she's wearing. I'm wondering how we'll ever wash it. It's even a struggle to get her to take it off at night."

Juana smiled. "Well, it's the one thing that belongs to her. Just give her time. Maybe when she feels at home and sees what the other little girls wear she'll decide to change." Then, as an afterthought, she added, "By the way, we haven't given this little one a name yet."

They discussed different possibilities and finally settled on the name Ruth. She'd be called Ruthie.

Juana and Marina went with Ellie to take the two little girls home. Arriving at the cottage set back in the trees, they were welcomed by several children who ran out to meet them. Rosita was holding Marina's hand, but another little girl about her age soon got her attention and drew her off to play. Ruthie, now awake, still clung to Juana.

Ellie and Marina both had a loving way with children. Juana and Marina stayed long enough for Ellie to make friends with Ruthie. There was an empty crib for her, and Juana gave her clothes and blankets from the storehouse. By the time Juana needed to leave, Ruthie was cradled in Ellie's arms, and Rosita was investigating her new bedroom with her new little sister. Children in the homes soon knew that they were part of a family with Mami, Papi, brothers, and sisters. When Juana and Marina walked back down the road, Juana breathed a sigh of relief. "I'm so glad that the little girls seemed comfortable when we left. They'll be fine with Ellie. Children always love her." Then changing the subject, she turned to Marina and said, "By the way, how are the two boys doing?"

"They are good little fellows and are trying to fit in with the family but, of course, they still feel strange. The older boy seems more outgoing. Salvador is very quiet." She shook her head. "It's obvious that they've gone through some terrible trauma. The general said their parents were killed but they haven't talked about it, and we haven't tried to get them to. Salvador, especially, has such a sad, pained expression in his eyes. I wish I knew how to reach him."

Juana nodded. "It's always hard to know just how to comfort children who have suffered the loss of their parents. Sometimes they cry a lot when they come, and I almost think it is better when they do, and not try to keep it all inside and suffer in silence. One thing we've learned is that they need love and security. They need to feel safe and permanent. The deeper wounds in their heart will take longer to heal, and of course there will always be scars. Do you think the boys have any religious background?"

"No, everything pertaining to religion, even asking the blessing at the table, seems foreign to them. They do what they're told to do, but I don't think they know anything about God."

"I can tell you that as they learn about their Father in heaven and how much He loves them it will bring a healing to them that nothing else can match. It never fails. These little abandoned children turn to God as naturally as flowers to the sun."

"I know, Juana. I've seen it with other children. They soon learn to love the Bible stories, and they especially love to sing."

"That's true!" Juana laughed. "In the early mornings and evenings when all the homes around the circle are celebrating worship, the children's voices just carry through the trees. Sometimes I feel that the angels must be joining them."

"I have noticed that Salvador, especially, enjoys singing," Marina said with a smile. "He is already learning the words to some of the songs."

"That's a good sign."

The two parted as they neared Marina's house, and Juana walked on alone. "I hope that Mami Fleck can come soon and see our new children," she murmured aloud. "She is always so happy when another abandoned child has been rescued."

Chapter (19)

*M*ama Fleck tells her story:

We first met Juana when she came to the Christian college where we were missionaries. She came from a typical Mayan home in the highlands of her country. Her sister-in-law brought her to our house, hoping to find work for her. During her two years with us we learned to love her as a daughter, and even after we left for another assignment we kept in touch and helped her stay in school. She learned quickly.

Of course, her background was very different from ours, but she adapted and became my right-hand helper. When I didn't need her any more, she worked at the college bakery and became a valued employee. But her help was invaluable in yet another area, and that would eventually decide her future.

Of all the needs I saw in the various fields where we served, my interest centered on needy and abandoned children. My husband, Ken, never knew when he might find some additions to our family and more little faces around the table. Juana loved to help me with these little children. One day I told her, "Juanita, if I ever start an orphanage, I'll send for you."

"I'll come and help you, señora. You can count on that."

Although neither Juana nor I really ever thought that would happen, it did. After a devastating earthquake Ken and I were asked to come to their country and help provide homes for the many orphaned children there. Thus International Children's Care was born.

Of course, I needed help. And I immediately thought of Juana.

Juana had just finished her education, and she was a natural. She started with ICC when we had only one home with 10 children. The need grew, and as one by one each house filled with children, God provided funds through the generosity of donors to build another.

"I don't know what we'd do without Juana," I told Ken one day as we walked down through the trees to one of the homes. "She is so responsible. And she really has a way with the children."

"Well," Ken replied, "God was no doubt preparing her for this long before we even thought about International Children's Care."

We were in our fourth year of operation when the general brought Salvador and the other children to El Bosque. When we started the homes we did not dream— nor could we have dreamed—that civil war would soon engulf this beautiful country, and that most of the children who came to us would be victims of that war.

Chapter 20

One evening Salvador and some of the other children were sitting around the living room, waiting for the call to supper when he overheard Papi Guillermo telling his wife a terrible tale. "Some new children came today. There were three children of one family—two little boys and their baby sister, about 2 years old. It seems that their father was an army officer, but they lived on a farm. The guerrillas first kidnapped their older brother, then came again and killed their mother. And just a few days ago they came back and killed their father. The boys were playing near the house and heard a shot down the road. They went running down there and found their father lying on the ground, dying."

"How terrible," she gasped. "Will this war never end?"

Salvador's heart began to pound as horrible pictures flashed through his mind. The day of his own loss. The day the soldiers killed his family.

At the table that evening Papi Guillermo told the children, "There are three new children in House Five. They've lost their parents, and they are very sad. We must remember to pray for them tonight."

But during the worship time and evening prayers, Salvador hardly heard what was being said. His mind was in a turmoil. He knew that while in the guerrilla army his family had fought against the military and done a lot of harm. But he'd been taught that they were justified in fighting for their lands, and that the army was the enemy to be destroyed. When he heard about three small children suffering because the guerrillas had killed their parents, he felt confused. Would those boys hate the people he had been defending the way he hated the army?

Salvador tossed and turned in his bed that night. He seemed to be back on the mountain, listening to the rhetoric of the guerrilla leaders. His mind raced, remembering vividly the stories of victories the adults recounted—the army camps attacked, the bridges blown up, truck loads of soldiers bombed. Then he would remember the final end to the dreadful period in his life when all of his family, except his father, was massacred. Tears spilled onto his pillow as he wrestled with the anguish and confusion in his young mind.

When the older of the two boys, Manuel, came to school the first time, Salvador watched him from the corner of his eye. At times he saw the boy's eyes fill with tears. In spite of the fact that their parents had been on opposite sides of the war, he felt Manuel's pain. Manuel was younger than he was, around 6 years old. The civil war was escalating, and the houses at the orphanage were filling up almost as fast as they could be built. Most of the children who came now were victims of that war. Some of them had seen one or both parents die, but all had become orphans with scars that would be with them forever.

As the days and weeks went by, Salvador became accustomed to the routine of El Bosque. He liked going to school. He began to make friends, but he never allowed himself to be intimate with anyone, and he never discussed his past life. First of all, it was too painful to talk about but, also, he still feared and hated the army. If anyone knew that his family had been guerrillas, he might still be in danger, or people would think bad of him. His mind stayed in a constant state of confusion, whirling with conflicting thoughts and emotions. But overall, he felt a smoldering anger at the world in general, and a basic distrust of everyone. "When I grow up, I'll avenge my parents," Salvador told himself again and again.

But the adults in his new life, Juana and his house parents, had no idea of the deep, dark thoughts that filled his heart. Although always reserved, quiet, and noncommittal, outwardly he was obedient and cooperative. He opened up most when the family sang the many choruses and songs during their family worships. All of the children loved to sing and did so with gusto. Lots of music and singing enhanced the church services too. "I don't believe all the things they say about God," Salvador would tell himself. "If He's such a good God, why do such bad things happen to people?" But he still looked forward to church meetings because of the music. And in spite of himself the words of the songs began to stay with him. Often he'd find himself singing as he worked or walked along the road to school.

One morning during the music period at school, the

teacher brought out some simple flutelike instruments and gave one to each child. "We're going to learn to play these flutes, and maybe we can even play them in church," she told them.

That really got Salvador's attention. He could hardly wait to learn to play a tune. Each day during music class they learned a few more notes and before long the children were able to play a simple tune. They were delighted. Now Salvador looked forward to music class. When they learned the song "Jesus Loves Me," they learned the words first, and then how to play the melody.

One Sunday morning Papi Guillermo announced, "We have some work to do today in our yard. If we hurry and get it done, we can join some of the other families to go to the river and swim this afternoon. How many will help me get the work done?"

All of the bigger children volunteered, including Salvador and Gaspar. They'd made a fence of sapling sticks to surround their ample yard. Today they'd clean the yard and cut the grass. Each boy was given a machete, and they all went to work. Salvador remembered that his father always carried a machete on the farm. It was used for lots of things, and Salvador enjoyed working as his father had done.

As soon as they finished their dinner and the dishes were washed and cleared away, Papi Guillermo called, "Everyone who wants to go to the river get your suit on. The pickup will be here soon to take us." When they heard the horn tooting out by the front gate the children ran out. Job was driving, and Juana was there to supervise the outing. She had provided every child with a swimming suit from clothes stored in the warehouse. The day was bright, and the afternoon sun shone down. It was a great day for swimming.

Salvador was anxious to go to the river, but he wasn't too sure about swimming. He hadn't learned to swim very well, even though he'd grown up playing in the stream where his mother did the laundry. It seemed a lifetime ago.

Some of the house fathers and older children walked on ahead. It was about a mile, over to the mission school property and on down to the river, still on the mission property. Guillermo, Salvador, and the older children in his house climbed into the back of the pickup. They were ready to go.

Most of the children had been to the river before, and as soon as they arrived they went running down the bank to the rocks and sandbar to join the rest of the group. The water was beautiful—clear and warm. It was shallow enough for an adult to walk across at that time of year. Trees lined the banks. Two brightly colored macaws that belonged to the mission school had followed the children. Each one perched high in a tree on opposite sides of the river, and their squawks added to the merriment of the day.

"Do you know how to swim?" Papi Guillermo asked Salvador, noticing that the boy just stood on the bank.

"Not very well. Is it deep?"

"No, not along here. Come on, son; I'll help you. Maybe you'll learn to swim today." Salvador was happy for the help. He cautiously waded in, taking Papi's hand. For the next two hours the children splashed and played.

Those who already knew how to swim spent their time jumping into the deeper parts and swimming out. Salvador stayed close to his new father, and soon found himself taking strokes. *This isn't hard!* he thought, *and the water feels so good. I wish we could come here every day!*

Finally Juana called, "It's time to go home. Everyone out!"

"Who wants to walk home with me?" Guillermo called. A group of the boys, including Salvador, joined him. As they walked down the dirt road toward home, Guillermo talked to the boys of many things. When they finally reached home, they were starved. Mami Marina had the table set and the supper waiting. Soon the lively group sat around the table. Most of the children were eager to tell Mami Marina about the great day at the river. Salvador ate quietly. He didn't join the others in telling about his day, but slowly he sensed a warm feeling creeping into his heart. After eating, everyone gathered for evening worship. It was a houseful of tired, happy children who gladly crawled into their beds that night.

After the candle was blown out Salvador lay in the dark, thinking over the day. It came to him that this was a good place to be. People were kind to him. It had been the best day he could remember for a long time.

Chapter 21

"Seño Juanita, Mami says to please come. It's Ruthie." One of the little girls from House Four stood at Juana's door. She was out of breath, for she had run all the way over.

"What's the problem?" Juana asked the child. "Is Ruthie sick?" The little girl had made great strides in the past few weeks, and Juana had felt sure she was on the mend.

"Yes, and she's crying and won't stop," the child tried to explain. Juana could see that she was distressed herself.

"Run back and tell Mami that I'll be right there," she said, hurrying to turn off the stove. Then she headed out the door and down the road toward the homes.

She heard Ruthie screaming as she neared the house. Ellie met her at the door. "Something is obviously hurting her, but I don't know what. She jabbers, but we can't understand her."

When Juana went to the crib, she began patting the child to try to quiet her, but the flow of sounds continued. Immediately Juana recognized that Ruthie was saying something in a dialect, but it was a different dialect from the one she understood.

Suddenly she had an idea. "Listen, Ellie. Ruthie is trying to tell us something. I remember that Salvador came from the same area as Ruthie. Maybe he can understand her. Let's send someone to find him."

Juana sent a boy to House One to find Salvador. Knocking on the back screen door, he relayed his message to Marina. "Seño Juanita wants Salvador."

"Oh, he isn't here. He's out working on the farm with Papi Guillermo and the other boys."

The messenger turned and went running down the road, past all the houses, and on out to the farm area. When he found the group weeding the new bean crop, he went to Guillermo. "Seño Juanita needs Salvador to come quick!"

Guillermo wondered what could be the reason for this request, but he didn't question it. "Salvador! They want you at House Four. It seems to be urgent."

Salvador dropped his hoe and ran back down the road. Juana met him at the door, and he could hear a child crying in the background. "I'm glad you came so soon, Salvador. Ruthie is trying to tell us something. See if you can understand her."

He hurried to the bedroom and leaned over the side of the crib. When he began to speak, it was not in Spanish or in the dialect that Juana understood, but Ruthie understood. She quit crying and began talking to Salvador. Soon he turned to the director. "Seño Juanita, she is saying that her throat hurts."

With his help translating, Juana succeeded in looking into the little girl's throat. It was inflamed. "We'll need to take her to the doctor again," she told Ellie. "I can see that she isn't really strong yet. She was so run-down. I'll make arrangements to take her right away."

With Salvador there the little girl quieted down. She and the boy continued talking in the unique dialect. When Ruthie had been taken to the doctor and Salvador went to leave, Juana stopped to ask him a question. "Did Ruthie come from the same place you did?"

"More or less," he answered carefully. "We understand the same language. Many small children don't speak Spanish."

By then Salvador was sure Ruthie was his cousin, Ana. He saw her at church or other occasions when the families were together. But he was still not willing to give any information about his background. Ruthie was too young to recognize him, and Juana had no idea that he was related, much less that he knew her family name. It seemed that during the weeks when he was tortured and threatened to try to force him to reveal information, his lips were sealed forever.

Chapter 22

*K*en and I had just come to El Bosque and were staying, as usual, in a travel trailer that we'd towed all the way down from Vancouver. In those beginning years it gave us a home away from home, for all of the housing was needed for the children. The trailer was parked near the director's apartment, and we took our meals with Juana.

We continued to be happy with Juana's leadership at El Bosque. She seemed to have the intuition needed to deal with the many children who came with numerous emotional problems as well as physical ones. Ken and I discussed her job performance as we walked along the path to her house for lunch.

I was so thankful for Juana. Besides her dedication to the children, she was industrious and efficient. "You know, she's really on call day and night," I told him. "If any of the mothers have problems with sick children, they send for her. Sometimes she needs to find someone to help her take a child into the hospital in the middle of the night."

"We'd be in real trouble if we didn't have someone

we could depend on," Ken added. "There must be at least 70 children here now."

It was true. There were really too many in most of the houses, but it was impossible to turn away children who didn't have anyplace else to go. We just prayed that we would be able to find the funds to build the rest of the houses we needed, and the school too.

As we ate, Juana brought us up to date on the most recent happenings. "After dinner, let's go and visit the homes," I suggested. "I'm eager to see the new children."

Ken decided to go with Job to see the farm, the newest construction, and whatever else he'd been doing while we met the new children. Then Juana had another idea. "I think you might like to visit one of the homes during their worship period tonight."

"We would really like that."

"I'd like to take you to House One," she said. "There are some special children there. You remember that the general brought six children in his helicopter? Yes. Well, two of those boys are in that home. The general said that they lost their families in a battle with the insurgents. The younger one, Salvador, is different from most of the others. He is very reserved and quiet, and hardly ever smiles. There's something mysterious about him. He is obedient and never causes trouble, but you just can't get close to him. And he's never talked about his family or his life before he came here."

"We can never know what these children have been through," I responded. "Anyway, I'm eager to see these boys. Let's plan to go. What time do we need to be there?"

"They eat their supper at 5:30, and worship is around 6:00."

"I'll see you then, if not before," Ken told us as he went out the door. "I think Job is outside waiting for me."

Salvador hadn't been at El Bosque long before he heard about Mami and Papi Fleck, and he was curious to know us. He'd heard that we loved the children and would do all we could for them. When the word was spread that "Mami and Papi Fleck are coming today!" Salvador wondered what we'd be like. He was curious, but he wasn't about to trust us any more than he did anyone else.

Juana and I spent a good part of the afternoon visiting in the homes. I loved becoming acquainted with many of the new children. Some of them were away from their houses in other activities, but the little ones, at least, were home with the mothers.

Juana had questions and some problems to discuss too. "We'll want to have a meeting with all the house parents and staff while you're here," she said as we walked back to the trailer. "Sometimes the parents have problems that I need help with. You know, we deal with so many different kinds of children—children from difficult backgrounds and who've suffered a lot of physical and emotional problems."

I nodded. "I'm sure, Juana, that this is even more of a challenging job than you imagined," I told her. "Just remember that you are helping Jesus in the person of these children. In a very special sense, they are God's children.

The Bible says that God is the Father of the fatherless. That really inspires me to do all I can for His children."

"That is the reason I'm here, Mami Fleck, and I thank you for bringing me here. I often feel unqualified for the job, but I just trust that God will help me in everything."

"I'm sure He will, Juana, and you can be sure that I pray for you every day."

At 6:00 that evening, Ken, Juana, and I sat in the living room of House One with a roomful of children and their house parents. The sun had just set, and darkness drops like a curtain in the tropics. Candles lit the room, and their flickering light gave a lovely atmosphere, casting a glow on the faces of the children. I counted them. There were 14, including Guillermo and Marina's small daughter. When Juana saw me counting, she leaned over to say, "I know we should not have more than 12 children to a house, but we're out of space. Marina always says to bring her an extra one if necessary."

"I understand," I replied. "Obviously she seems to be handling it well."

Ken and I recognized some of the children. There were three little sisters I'd seen before—Julia, Amanda, and Reina. Their mother had died, and for a while their father struggled to keep them together. But he couldn't work and care for them too. Eventually he heard of El Bosque, a Christian home for children, and he brought them. The youngest one, Reina, managed to sit next to me, snuggling up close.

"My children, we have visitors tonight," Guillermo began. "Mami and Papi Fleck are with us. Let's go around the circle and everyone tell them your name. They want to know you."

When Salvador's turn came, his voice was barely audible. "Salvador Gomez, to serve you," he murmured.

I thought of what Juana had told me about Salvador, so I made it a point to affirm him. "I'm so happy to know you, Salvador. We're glad that you've come to live here."

The children enthusiastically sang several songs. They knew all the words. Salvador seemed to brighten up during the singing, and he sang too. But when Guillermo began to tell the Bible story and went over the memory verse for the day, I could see that Salvador pulled back. It was as if he closed himself off from the others, and off from the Word of God.

Two of the children prayed as they closed their worship, then they all came to tell us good night. Salvador stayed behind the others, seeming to hesitate, but Ken gave him a big hug and a hearty pat on the back. Then I took the little fellow in my arms with a special squeeze, telling him quietly, "I'm so glad you are here, Salvador. I'm so sorry for all you have lost. I just want you to know that you are safe here. We love you, and Jesus loves you too."

I felt pensive as some time later Juana, Ken, and I walked down the road beneath a sky brilliant with stars. I thought of the struggle I'd gone through in the decision to take on the responsibility of an orphange. But as I pondered all the homes full of children—innocent children who had suffered the results of sin in our harsh, chaotic world—my heart was full. I couldn't help exclaiming aloud, "What beautiful, precious children. This is what International Children's Care is all about—a haven for these poor little ones. What if one of mine had been left alone like they were!"

When the last candle went out around the circle of homes and there were only the night noises of the jungle, I stepped outside the trailer door and stood looking up into the sky. Out there, so far from city lights, the stars hung like clusters of jewels in the heavens. I lifted my heart to God. *Dear Father, thank You for letting us do this for You. Thank You for every one of these little children. Please help us know how to teach them about You. Give Juana wisdom and strength and Your kind of love for these children. Bless every house parent. These are Your children. Help us to never forget it.*

Chapter 23

*T*he next morning as Ken and I were discussing the day's plans with Juana our conversation turned to the recent upset in government. It was a topic that interested and concerned everyone. "Have you heard anything about where General García is these days?" Ken inquired. "I remember that he bought a farm in the area when he was the commander of the base here."

"We haven't seen him, but I heard that he's living back on his farm. Of course, he would have a right to retirement benefits," Juana explained. "I guess he's an ordinary civilian now, with his party out of control."

"I thought he might have come out to see the children, especially those six he himself brought recently," I mused. "I wonder how Salvador and Gaspar would feel about seeing him again."

"I'm afraid seeing him would bring back bad memories," Juana replied, passing the toast around again. "But I don't doubt that the general will be out before long. When he was commander here he liked to visit the children, and they always crowded around him."

"Yes, I remember that one time he told us that he loves children and animals," Ken added. "I always thought that was an unusual comment from a tough army general."

"It will be interesting to see Salvador's reaction when the general does come," Juana said. "I have a feeling that Salvador's story is not just about losing his parents."

General García had moved back to his farm. And even though he was now a civilian he continued to be involved with the children, often finding another orphan that needed help. He'd brought many children to El Bosque, but there seemed to be something special about Salvador to him, for he always kept his eye on him. He must have heard about the unusual little boy who stood up to everyone for what he thought was his duty. Little did anyone realize then the role that General García would play in Salvador's life.

Days turned into weeks and weeks into months. The seasons changed, and one lonely, angry little boy learned to fit into the program in his home and in the school. Salvador was obedient and cooperative, but it was only a cover. In his mind raged a storm so intense that, at times, he thought of running away. But he was a practical, logical boy, and because he'd come in by air he had no idea where he was. Thus, he didn't know where he could go.

There was nothing for him to do but bide his time. He could be patient. "I'll just have to wait until I'm older," he told himself. "But someday I'll get away and avenge my father's death."

Nights were the worst. On his bed in the quiet darkness he tossed and turned, terrible images of the past tumbling through his mind. When sleep finally came, it was almost worse, for in sleep the dreams returned. He dreamed of his childhood, of green fields, and happy days with his parents. These joyful scenes were scrambled with other pictures in his mind—the camp, the cruelty he'd been taught, the times that he himself had been involved in violence.

Again and again he relived the night on the mountain when all of the camp escaped except him. He felt the terror. The loneliness. The sense of utter abandonment. There was the momentary exhilaration when he'd made his way home and thought his family was there.

And finally, the horror beyond words when his family was massacred. There in his sleep his mind replayed what he repressed by day, and his screams of terror would fill the little house. During one of those nightmares his screams awakened his house parents. Guillermo ran into Salvador's room and found him sobbing and writhing in his bed. "What's the matter, Salvador? Wake up! It's only a dream!" The father took the little boy in his arms and held and caressed him. "Tell me, son, what is it?"

"*Mi mamá! Mi papá!*" he cried.

Marina had come to his room by then, and Guillermo told her, "It's the dreams about his parents." As they saw the child's intense trauma and grief, their own eyes filled with tears. He'd never breathed a word of his story. They only knew that his pain was too deep for words.

Back in their room, Guillermo told his wife, "Only God can heal a grief like that. We must find a way to help him to know his Father in heaven."

But gradually there began to be times—especially during the day—when Salvador almost felt happy. He was still a child. He loved to play ball with the boys. The excursions to the river were highlights, and he became an excellent swimmer, diving off the rocks over and over again with the rest of the boys. After days of heavy exertion, he slept better, though still plagued by dreams.

All of the house mothers at El Bosque knew the birth dates of the children they cared for. In some cases when the birthday of an abandoned child was unknown, they were assigned one. Salvador knew that his birthday was November 15, but he had not told his house parents. However, Juana had asked him his birth date when he first came, and had given it to Marina. So on November 15 the rest of the family planned a surprise celebration for Salvador.

When everyone had finished eating that evening, Mami Marina came to the table carrying a beautifully decorated cake, all lit with candles. *"Cumpleaños feliz!"* ("Happy birthday") she called out, and everyone began to sing "Happy birthday to Salvador." It was an emotional moment for him, his first birthday cake since the happy days on the farm in his childhood. It was also one small step in the emotional healing that had slowly begun. At last he was learning to feel like part of this new family.

There were presents for him, too—some simple ones from the other children in the home, and one from his house parents, actually provided by the office in Vancouver.

The next big event was Christmas. For days Juana and her helpers had been unpacking boxes that came in a shipment from Vancouver. Besides the many necessary supplies, there were toys, appropriate for each age, as well as new articles of clothing. As she sorted and organized, she set aside special things for Christmas. Then there came the task of personalizing the gifts for each child and wrapping them in Christmas paper. Eighty children lived at El Bosque by then. As the big day drew near, the fathers and boys cut pine trees from the nearby forest and in each home the children set up their own tree. Juana provided some decorations, and the children made more simple ones. Thus, the trees were beautifully festive. And although they were in the tropics and had no prospect of snow, it began to look and feel like Christmas.

Besides the tree, sponsors and donors provided funds to purchase special provisions for the Christmas feast. It would not be Christmas in that country without the traditional Christmas tamales. When the children came in for their dinner, Salvador noticed the banana leaves and other ingredients for the tamales sitting on the table. He didn't want to ask, but one of the other children shouted, "Goody! Christmas tamales!" A small, warm feeling crept into Salvador's heart. It had been so long since the carefree days when his mother made Christmas tamales!

Tamales were made in huge kettles with finely ground corn and rice that had been cooked to the consistency of hot cereal. The cook placed a spoonful of the cooked meal on a large banana leaf she held in her hand. To this were added dried prunes, green olives, pimientos, pieces of vegetarian meat, and then a special spicy tomato sauce over it all. Then the banana leaf was wrapped up, tied with string, and placed in a huge kettle. When the kettle was full, they were cooked until the flavors had blended. In addition to the tamales were Christmas cakes and special fruits that could only be afforded once a year, especially apples and grapes.

For some of the children it was their first Christmas, and they were wide-eyed with excitement and fun. For Salvador, it was indeed the first for many years. When Christmas Eve arrived, the candles were lit, the base of the tree was piled high with presents, and a Christmas spirit filled the air. Deep inside his heart, Salvador began to sense something that felt strange to him. Although he didn't really realize it, he was beginning to feel like part of this family—it was a good, warm feeling. He, along with the other children, looked longingly at the stack of presents and wondered if it held something for him.

After supper that evening, Papi Guillermo called the family to the living area. The light from the candles brought from the kitchen flickered on the faces of the children. Guillermo told the story of the Babe in Bethlehem. It was a first for Salvador. No one had ever told him the story like that before. He couldn't comprehend it all, nor was he sure he wanted to believe it, but a light began to flicker in his mind, in spite of himself.

After the Christmas story they sang carols. These were new to Salvador, but he listened carefully, hoping he could learn these beautiful songs. Then they all knelt to pray to this God and His Son, who had come as a baby to this world.

When the prayer was over, Mami Marina announced, "It's time now to see what we have under the tree!" The children squealed with excitement, and the fun began. Soon Salvador heard his name. "I think Santa has something for a boy named Salvador. Where is he?" And Salvador jumped up and went up for his present.

"Open it, son," Papi said with a big smile. "It's for you!" When the boy pulled the wrapper away, he found a new T-shirt—red with white stripes. Salvador looked at it with shining eyes. It was brand new, and it was his.

One by one, each child heard his or her name and went for their present. Then to his surprise, Salvador heard his name again. He hadn't expected two presents. This time he unwrapped a game. Every child had two presents. One was something to wear, and another was a toy.

When the last package had been opened, the room was full of paper and new toys. It was an excited, happy group who finally got into their pajamas and crawled into bed. Salvador quickly fell asleep and knew nothing more until he was awakened at dawn by the rooster outside his window. He had not dreamed.

Chapter 24

*T*wo years went by and Salvador felt at home in his new environment, but the old dreams and terrors still shattered his nights. He trusted his house parents and Juana, but a passion for vengeance still festered in his heart.

Yet as he listened to the Bible stories and learned more and more about the God of love, he realized that his emotions and feelings were in conflict with the new concepts he was beginning to believe were true. But he had questions. *How could such terrible things have happened if God really is love?* He didn't yet know the answer, but now he wanted to be free of the negative, hateful thoughts.

Ken and I spent as much time as possible at El Bosque, and I learned to know the children personally. Salvador was always friendly and respectful and seemed happy to see us. There was always something different about him, and at times I could see in his eyes the sadness and pain hovering beneath the surface. But outwardly, he seemed well adjusted.

The children understood that Ken and I—Mami and

Papi Fleck to them—had founded and now directed the program that gave them a home, food, and security. Whenever we arrived, they came running, hugging and kissing us, and we loved them all. Salvador, though not as aggressive as some, was always there for his share of our attention. I tried to keep up with the progress of the children, and each time, I could see that Salvador seemed more secure and at home.

Morning and evening worships were brief, but geared to a child's understanding, especially to children with no basis in religion or the Bible. By morning a Bible verse was read—verses with special meaning for children, such as John 3:16: "'For God so loved the world, that he gave his only begotten Son . . .'" Then Papi Guillermo gave a simple explanation.

The story of God's gift to the world was always of intense interest to the children. The idea of a living God—Creator of heaven and earth—sending His Son to this earth to save them, and of God's interest in each of them, did much to fill the void in their hearts. Salvador could relate to the story of the cruelty Jesus suffered. *People did terrible things to people then too*, he thought. *If Jesus was treated like that, maybe He knows how I feel.* That thought turned on a light in the boy's mind. Papi Guillermo had told them that Jesus hears when we pray and He understands us and our needs. In the quiet of his own mind Salvador pondered such a mystery.

One evening at the family gathering, Papi Guillermo announced that a Bible study class was going to be held before the church service on Sunday evenings. Anyone who would like to learn more about the Bible could go.

"I'm sure you still have many questions," he told his family. "For instance, we've all wondered how there can be so much bad in the world if God is love and if He's truly all-powerful. These classes will help you to understand that and many other things. Think about it, and speak to the pastor if you'd like to enroll."

Salvador pricked up his ears. The question of bad in the world was the problem that nagged him the most. Unlike most children, he had *lived* it. His family had been drawn into it, almost without choice. And so he determined to join the class. By now he'd learned to pray a simple prayer, but it was more form than anything else. He still did not know how to open his heart to God.

For the first few weeks of class Salvador listened quietly, but nothing escaped his notice. While he worked on the farm, while he sat in school, and especially in his bed alone at night, he pondered the things he was learning. The story of Lucifer and his rebellion against God and subsequent fall was a shock and revelation. So *that's* where evil came from! When he learned of the extent of Satan's fury against the Son of God, and his determination to take control, Salvador began to understand what prompted people to do the wicked and depraved things he had lived through. He began to realize that each of us must make a decision. Whose side are we on?

Week after week the stories of the Bible showing God's true character, and especially His great love for every single person in the world, began to take root in Salvador's heart. Again he thought through the events he and his family experienced. He relived his years at the rebel camp, his escape, his capture and torture, and then his rescue. He pondered these things in relation to the things he was learning. Could it be that it was God who had rescued him the day of the massacre, when he was pulled out of the line of death? Could it even be that it was in God's providence that the captain rescued him again, giving him a new name? During those weeks of classes he learned that prayer is simply talking to God as to a close and personal friend, and something new gripped his heart—a desire to know this God better.

There were many things to learn. One evening the pastor teaching the class announced a surprise. "Those of you who have not missed a class have earned a Bible of your own."

Salvador's heart beat faster with excitement. He knew that he'd attended every class. When the pastor handed him the Bible, he took it reverently. "Thank you, Pastor. Thank you so much!" At that moment he sensed the sacredness of the book, and it became his most precious possession.

Week after week he studied, reading the age-old stories for himself. Page after page he discovered things he'd never comprehended. He learned how he could be forgiven—that claiming the blood of Jesus shed on Calvary he could be free of all the guilt of his past. No one but him knew the deep, dark secrets in his heart; all the people he had hurt and even killed. *Is it possible that God can forgive all this?* he asked himself, awed at the thought. He learned how to claim God's promises of power to overcome Satan and live a new life in Christ.

His new understanding, what the Bible teaches about the dead was a comfort to him. He read in his Bible that the dead are asleep and know nothing until awakened at the second coming of Jesus. He'd struggled with the thought that his mother, and possibly his father—though dead—were still somewhere. That they knew or saw all he did and how he had suffered. Now he understood that they rested in their graves.

Ever since coming to El Bosque three years before, Salvador had attended services with the rest of the children on the seventh-day Sabbath. Now he learned why it was important to worship on that day. He learned that God made the Sabbath as a memorial to the creation of our world. He learned that the Sabbath was a gift of time to us, a day to honor and remember God even as we rest from our labor. From then on the seventh-day Sabbath had deep meaning for Salvador.

As he pondered all of these new things he realized that these thoughts were replacing the torment that had tortured his mind for so long. Maybe there was yet hope for him!

Finally one night he knelt down beside his bed, his face in his hands. Tears fell down his cheeks as he prayed, "Dear Father in heaven. I don't know You very well yet, but I long to know You better. I want You to take out all of the hateful thoughts in my mind and teach me how to believe and trust You. Please help me!"

It was a turning point in his life. To his surprise, he began to sleep through the night, deep, sweet sleep. His obsession with vengeance grew less and less as the Bible stories and the love of Jesus filled his mind, replacing the consuming, bitter desire for revenge.

During the months of Bible study classes, Papi Guillermo often came into his room at bedtime to talk over with him the things he heard in the class. This new father was the one that Salvador went to with questions, and Guillermo often knelt with him beside his bed and prayed with him. Salvador felt a deep hunger to know God better. Could it really be that there was a solution to the torment of his soul, a hope for the future, and something to live for? It was the beginning of a friendship with God that would change his life. For the first time since his father joined the rebels he began to feel real happiness and security.

By the time Salvador had attended Bible classes for a year, the pastor taught them that Jesus gave us an example by being baptized in the river Jordan. Baptism was a way of showing an end to our old life and the beginning of a life with Him. When the pastor asked those who would like to be baptized to stay for a special prayer, Salvador stayed.

The meetings continued, and now Salvador went eagerly looking forward to the day when he could follow the example of the One he had learned to love and trust. Deep inside, a strong feeling told him that this was something he must do. This was the answer to his problems.

Finally a date was set for the baptism. It would be on a Sabbath afternoon, and held down in the beautiful river that ran through the jungle on the mission property. Salvador felt especially thrilled when it was announced that "Mami and Papi Fleck will be here next week for the baptism. Since Papi Fleck is a pastor of many years of experience, he will do the baptizing." That news made everything perfect. Salvador and the rest of the young people awaiting baptism eagerly looked forward to the day.

We arrived at El Bosque on Thursday, and that evening Ken met with those planning to be baptized. He spent some time talking personally with each one of them. Salvador sensed the sacredness of this step. "Baptism signifies a death and burial to your old life, and the beginning of your new life with Christ," Ken told them. Ken felt confident in their decisions, for each student had been carefully instructed and prepared. Each recognized the seriousness and import of their decision.

That Friday night Guillermo went to Salvador's bedside to tell him good night, and to have one last visit before this significant day. "I just want you to know, son, that I am happy and proud of you. I'm sure that you will look back on tomorrow—the day of your baptism—as one of the most important days of your life. And I feel certain that God has a special plan for your life. If you let Him lead you, you will know what that plan is."

Although Salvador, now a young teen, had looked forward to baptism as a necessary step in the solution to his mental turmoil, he could not realize that it would completely change the direction of his life.

As the years had passed, Guillermo and Marina had grown more aware of the trauma that haunted Salvador's heart. They felt certain that he had suffered terribly at the loss of his parents, but they'd never heard his story. Salvador would never forget the love and comfort his new parents had given him as his screams awakened him from the nightmares. He would always remember what their love and acceptance had meant to him during those painful years, and how their loving concern and their prayers gave him a glimpse of the love of his heavenly Father.

That day at the river would never be forgotten—not only by Salvador, but by many of the children. It was a landmark for Ken and me, too, for it was the first baptism conducted at El Bosque. My heart thrilled as I stood on the shore in the shade of the giant jungle trees. Not only were all the children and their house parents there, but many of the teachers and students of the mission school. A shelter had been made of sheets so the candidates had privacy to change clothes. One of the house fathers led the crowd in singing such songs as "Shall We Gather at the River?" "Whiter Than Snow," and "I Surrender All."

Then Ken walked out into the just the right spot in the river and began to speak. "This is a special day in the lives of these young people. They have decided to cast their lot with the One who died for them, and with the One who has promised to prepare them homes, not temporary ones, but homes for eternity. God has had a hand in bringing each of them to this place and to this moment. From this time forward, they will belong to the Lord who loves the children and said, 'Come unto Me.'" Then Ken lifted his arms to lead the crowd in prayer, asking God's presence on that occasion.

There was silence in the crowd. Only the gentle ripple of the water, the birds in the trees, and the rustle of the wind in the leaves were heard. *Could it have been something like this that day at the Jordan River?* I wondered. *There must be angels surrounding this place.*

Juana, in a white dress, stepped into the river to help the young people, one by one, go to Ken. She was there with a sheet to wrap around them as they came out of the water, their faces shining with happiness.

As Salvador's turn came, his heart overflowed with an emotion too deep for words. Although only in his early teens, life had already handed him experiences far too heavy for his tender age. His thoughts were deep as pictures flashed through his mind—especially the scene at his father's ranch when his whole family was killed at the hands of the enemy. He could still feel the captain taking him by the front of his shirt and pulling him from the line. During the past few months he'd relived that day many times, wondering why he—of all his family—had been snatched from death. Instead of the anger and grief that had plagued him for so long, the conviction had grown in his mind that God took a hand in his life that day. He alone had been saved—and for a purpose.

Then Ken raised his hand, saying, "I now baptize you in the name of the Father, the Son, and the Holy Spirit." As he gently laid him back beneath the warm, clear water, Salvador felt totally embraced in the love and peace of God. Those on the bank sang again as this child of God emerged from the water and walked toward Juana.

He'd always remember the sensation he felt in that moment, that the heavy burden he'd carried for so long was lifted from his shoulders. The old depression, anger, and even grief, were gone, replaced with a new sense of peace and security. At last the battle that had waged in his heart for so long had been won. Although he did not know if his earthly father was dead or alive, he knew for certain that his heavenly Father, the Creator and ruler of the universe, lived, and that he was now a child of God. His happiness was beyond description.

After the service, Salvador stood on the shore with the other newly baptized young people, receiving the welcome into God's family from those in attendance. I came up to him and wrapped him in my arms. "God bless you, son. We are so happy for you today. May this be a day you will never forget. We are so glad you are part of our family here, and now that you have decided to be part of the great family of God."

Chapter 25

"How are all the children doing?" Juana asked as she made her morning rounds in the homes. She enjoyed spending time with the house mothers.

"Come in, Señorita Juana," Marina invited, leading the director to their living area. "Please sit down."

The house mothers enjoyed Juana's visits, for she had a friendly relationship with each one and they looked to her for counsel and guidance. "I've been noticing a difference in Salvador the past few weeks—since his baptism," Juana said as the two women sat down. "He is one boy that's been hard to get next to, and yet I've never heard complaints about him from anyone. However, lately he seems happier. He's smiling more and acting more like a boy his age should act."

"It's true," Marina agreed. "He doesn't have nightmares anymore. He's sleeping through the night, and just acts different. Guillermo has tried to keep close to him, and although Salvador never wants to talk about his past now he's much more open about his feelings about God. He's taking an active part in our morning and evening worships, too. He seems eager to learn the memory verses, and he's asking questions." She smiled, adding, "And, of course, he loves to sing."

"I'm so glad to hear that. I'm always concerned about these children who come from tragic circumstances." Juana sighed. "Of course, most of them do, but Salvador's case has seemed different from that of the others. I've been very concerned about his being so withdrawn."

"Guillermo wants to take our children—and any others who want to go—to do missionary work in a nearby area," Marina told her. "There's a village near here that has no church."

Juana nodded. "Yes, he's talked to me about it, and I think it's a great idea. I'll try to arrange for transportation. It will be a nice outing for Sabbath afternoons."

"Thank you, Señorita Juanita. The children will be excited. They've been practicing songs to sing, and Guillermo wants to hold meetings and invite the village people. The children can visit the homes, inviting the people to come."

After worship a few days later, the plans complete, Guillermo asked if anyone would like to go with him to a nearby village. "You will visit the people and tell them about Jesus," he said.

"Me! Me! Me!" they all shouted. "When are we going?"

"This very next week!"

That was the beginning. Week after week the children were taught to share what they'd learned—and experienced—about their heavenly Father in heaven. Nearly every Sabbath afternoon a group went to a neighboring village. Besides helping with the music and visiting the homes to invite people to the meetings, the older children learned how to give simple Bible studies. In a gentle, simple way, they told what they knew about God and His plan for His children in this world. The village people looked forward to seeing them week after week, and the crowds at the little meeting increased. Soon there was a nucleus to organize a church.

Salvador was one of the most enthusiastic, for *he* had something to share. He had experienced the healing power of God for himself. And in addition to visiting and giving Bible studies, Salvador became more and more involved in the music the students provided for the meetings. "Salvador is becoming a leader in our missionary work," Guillermo told Juana one day as he brought her up to date on the Sabbath ministry. "I think that boy has real potential. Whatever he does, he puts his heart in it. And he's developing into quite a singer."

Salvador also became more and more active in the services at El Bosque. He learned to speak in public, but he specially loved to help with music. With his increasing responsibilities in the spiritual life at El Bosque, his studies, as well as sports and work, kept him busy.

He'd been at El Bosque for five years when a blow came that brought a new kind of sadness. For personal reasons, Guillermo and Marina were going to leave. It wasn't an easy decision on their part, especially so as they knew the impact it could have on "their" children. It was always hoped that house parents would stay and become permanent substitute parents. However, situations sometimes arose that made it impossible, and new parents had to be found. Salvador had accepted this kind couple as second parents, and he loved and respected them. Guillermo was a good father. He believed in discipline but he reasoned with the children before punishment, helping them to understand the reasons. Juana knew it would not be easy to replace them, and that the children would feel the loss.

She made temporary arrangements until she could find another couple. Most of the children seemed to take the change in stride, but Salvador deeply felt the loss of Papi Guillermo. He accepted the change as necessary, but inwardly decided that he would never allow himself to get so attached to the house parents again, since they might not stay.

Finally the new parents came. Donaldo and his wife were teachers, but, loving children, they decided to accept this new role as house parents. Salvador soon learned to trust and respect the new house father. However, he never called him Papi, as the others did. To Salvador, he remained Professor.

Of course, Donaldo's personality was different from Guillermo's, but being a teacher he understood children. He sensed that Salvador was a boy of deep feelings and thoughts, and they quickly developed a strong friendship. And as the years passed, besides being his house father, Donaldo eventually became Salvador's best friend.

A year went by quickly, and Salvador was happy. He was doing well in school, and Donaldo often helped him with his homework. But this was not to last. Donaldo's wife grew ill. The responsibility of mothering 12 children was too much for her, and the doctor insisted she must give up the position.

Though they'd served as house parents only a year, their leaving was a loss—especially to Salvador. He felt he was losing a valuable friend. By that time, however, he was an integral part of El Bosque. The school, his friends, and of course Juana, gave him a deep sense of security. And even though Donaldo left El Bosque, he did not forget the children. He especially kept in touch with Salvador, occasionally sending him letters to encourage him.

Salvador sometimes looked back to his baptism. From that day forward, the nightmares had disappeared. So had the hateful, bitter feelings that had haunted him for so long. Giving his heart to God had been a breakthrough. It had freed him to wholeheartedly take part in the normal school routines as well as to do missionary work and participate in special programs such as Pathfinders and music. Music was his first love. As his voice developed, the leaders realized he had unusual talent, and he often sang solos as well as singing with the group.

When Salvador and his classmates graduated from primary school, a new world opened up for them. Now they were no longer children, but young people. For the first three years they walked to the mission secondary school about half a mile away.

At the beginning of the next school year Juana asked Salvador if he'd like to move into the boy's dormitory at school. "I know you're involved in many activities and it might be easier to live there," she told him.

For a moment the boy stood looking at the floor without answering. "You know, Seño Juanita, I love living in my home," he said after thinking it over, "but it would probably be easier to be closer. I could still come home to visit, couldn't I?"

"Of course you could, just like the other older students do. You don't have to decide right now. Think it over and let me know."

Before classes started in the new school year, Salvador moved into the boys dorm, rooming with some friends from El Bosque. And more and more, he distinguished himself with his active participation in all school activities, but especially in music. He formed a men's quartet that became the official quartet of the school.

On one of my visits to El Bosque, I left my trailer to walk to the Sabbath morning service at the school community. I enjoyed being there. Besides the fact that it was unique as a children's church, it was an outdoor church. A bamboo shelter with a palm branch roof—typical of the country—stood in the parklike area of El Bosque. This area was surrounded by a circle of the children's homes. The shelter was a model of beautiful native craft, the beams made of natural trees. A platform had been built at the front of the church. Its backdrop was a bamboo wall with a large painting of Jesus' baptism. Each week a different house of children decorated their church with flowers and palm branches. When visitors were expected, a special touch was added—pine needles covered the entire floor. Simple wooden pews furnished ample seating space for the more than 100 children and staff. The church was open on three sides and surrounded by a flowering hibiscus hedge.

From the moment that I left my trailer I heard beautiful music coming over the church's loud speaker. *Where did they get that tape, and who is singing?* I wondered. But as I got near the entrance, I saw that it was Salvador singing! Even though he was now an academy student, he loved to visit his home church at El Bosque.

In the interval between services, I noticed the quartet standing out under the trees practicing, and I stepped closer to listen. Salvador was directing them. Although they had no accompaniment, he was drilling one of the students with his part. Even as he sang, Salvador could hear each part and could tell if one of them missed a note. Then he would stop and sing that part with the other boy until he felt it was learned. I was amazed. With my own background in music, I wondered, "With no formal education in music, how can he do this?" When they sang at the second service it was beautiful.

That evening Juana came to my trailer to talk over some of her concerns, and the hour grew late as we talked through some problems. All of the 10 homes full of children were now quiet, and the generator had been turned off. My gas lantern provided the only light.

Suddenly we heard a movement outside the trailer. Juana jumped up, alarmed. After all, there was still a civil war, and terrorists had been known to be in the area. She called out, *"Quien es?"* ("Who is it?")

To our surprise, we heard, *"El quarteto!"*

We opened the door, and there stood the four boys! "We came to give Mami Fleck a *serenata,* and we couldn't wait any longer for her to go to sleep!" After all, a serenade is supposed to blend in with your dreams and wake you up.

Juana and I went out to the patio in front of the trailer and sat in the lawn chairs to hear the concert—and it was a *concert!* I couldn't keep back the tears as they sang. They all gave me a hug as they left, but Salvador lingered. "Mami Fleck, thank you for coming, and thank you for all you and all of the ICC family have done for us. You will never know what it has meant to me!"

Chapter 26

*T*he years passed rapidly. Salvador continued to mature into·a stable, solid Christian young man. Beyond secondary education, the school offered a teacher's course. Because of his deep admiration and continuing friendship with Donaldo, teaching seemed the logical goal for him. "I'm not sure I want to always be a teacher," he told Donaldo. "But at least I can always make a living teaching, and I like to work with children." Donaldo and his wife had returned to El Bosque, and this time he was director of the four-teacher primary school.

"You'll make a good teacher," his friend told him. "And God will guide you in your future if you allow Him to."

The missionary trips continued. Although many of the younger children were included, most often the pastor looked to the older students who lived in the dormitories at the mission school. Salvador and two girls, Mayra and Amali, formed a trio. Each had been blessed with a beautiful voice. Salvador sang tenor, Mayra contralto, and Amali soprano. Their trio became so popular that they spent a lot of time practicing for special occasions and often went on missionary trips together. It soon became apparent that Salvador and Mayra were more than just friends. Besides their common interest in music, they had another common bond.

Mayra was from an isolated village. And during the height of the civil war a band of guerrillas attacked the village early one morning, killing every man they could find. In a few short minutes her father, grandfather, and uncles were killed. Along with 11 of her siblings and cousins, she was brought to El Bosque. Mayra and Salvador had both experienced real tragedy. They'd gone through grade school together, each a part of an El Bosque family. During those years Salvador didn't notice girls, but he and Mayra grew up as friends.

During the last year of their teacher's training, students needed three months of teaching practice in a primary school. So every day Salvador and a group from his class went by bus to a school in a neighboring town. He taught a class of 53 children. The director noticed a marked difference between the practice teachers that came from the mission school and those from other schools. One day some parents approached Salvador. "We wish that you students from the mission school were teaching here all the time. You have such different methods. The children aren't afraid of you. They look forward to your classes. They say you never threaten them, but tell them how well they are doing."

Another day one of the regular teachers in the school spoke to Salvador. "I wish you would tell me your secret. Your classes are orderly, and the students seem to obey you so well. I threaten and threaten and punish, but it doesn't seem to help."

Salvador tried to give the young man some pointers, but in his heart he felt that God was giving him special wisdom and help with his classes. He found teaching a joy for him as well as a challenge. Often, even during his classes, the thought flashed through his mind, *I feel chosen by God. I feel His presence with me.* And then another scene would follow, that of a little boy being roughly jerked out of a line, a line of death. No longer did that memory bring back the horror and bitterness. Instead, he felt a deep sense of God's special intervention in his life. *I know for sure that God has something special in life for me. When the captain told me that he was giving me his name with the hope that I could save someone, he little knew what he was doing.*

Salvador often thought about that final day at his father's ranch. He could almost feel the rough hands on the front of his shirt. His changed heart from the former obsession of horror to peace and thankfulness was a constant reminder that he was a special child of God.

As graduation day drew nearer he grew preoccupied with the question "What does God want me to do?" He knew of a school that needed a teacher, but his confidence in God's leading was so strong that he felt he should wait for a special invitation instead of applying.

General García, now retired to private life in the village near El Bosque, had built a beautiful home. He'd recently been elected mayor of the small town, which included the surrounding area. On occasion he visited El Bosque and the mission school, and often asked to see

Salvador. Although he'd brought other children to El Bosque through the years, he seemed particularly interested in this boy. And although Salvador remembered the general as the one who brought him, no mention had ever been made about his family or background.

One afternoon General García stopped by Juana's office and asked to talk to her. He didn't take long to get to the object of his visit. "You know I've had an interest in Salvador Gomez ever since I brought him to you years ago in my helicopter. And as I've seen this institution grow and watched you and the children, I have been more and more impressed with the quality of what you are doing. I'm so thankful that something is being done for these children who have been victims in our country."

Juana listened attentively as he went on. "I have been looking for a young man to hire for my office. He needs to be absolutely honest and trustworthy, because he will be one of the officials in the Treasury Department. I keep thinking about Salvador. Would you consent to letting me offer him the job?"

"General García, Salvador is a young man of age now. He has good judgment and can make his own decision. You are free to talk to him."

"Thank you, Juana. I'll drive right on over to the college and see if I can find him." And he was gone.

Salvador was surprised at the general's proposal. It really wasn't what he expected that God had in mind for him. But he thought, *Mami Fleck wrote to the graduates that the administration of ICC believed that those wanting help with their advanced education should work for a year first. This would be a good job, and maybe I can be a witness in that place.*

He'd never lived anywhere except at El Bosque or in the mission school dormitory. When the general offered him the choice of having a house of his own in the town or living on the farm with him, he chose the house in town.

The next week, after graduation, he packed up his things to be ready when the general came for him. He was shocked when he stepped into his new home. It was a large house—completely furnished. And it was to be his! He knew it would be a challenge to purchase his own groceries and cook his own food, but the idea wasn't too frightening, since all the children at El Bosque learned to help with household chores. Many of the boys even learned to bake bread and prepare meals. He unpacked his clothes in one of the bedrooms and hung them in the closet, and he was home.

Chapter 27

"You know, Salvador, our home is yours," his old friend, Professor Donaldo, told him after he'd moved to town to work for the general. "We have an extra room that you can call your own. Plan to spend your weekends here with us." As director of the grade school at El Bosque, Donaldo and his family lived in one of the faculty homes.

Salvador smiled. "Thank you, Prof. I do feel at home at your house, and I love it here at El Bosque. I'll just take you up on that offer. I still want to be involved in the church here and especially in the missionary trips."

Salvador bought a secondhand bicycle, and every Friday afternoon he could be seen pedaling along through the jungle out to El Bosque. He always arrived in time for supper with the family. Donaldo's children loved Salvador like an older brother, and his friendship with the teacher deepened almost to that of father and son.

"Tell us about your work, Salvador," Donaldo said one Friday evening at the supper table.

"Well, it is really a new experience for me, Prof. I'm still learning, but I enjoy it. The general calls me his son and couldn't treat me better." He sat thoughtfully for a moment. "I'm trying hard to not disappoint him, since he's shown so much confidence in me. He says he knows he doesn't have to worry about funds that I take care of."

"I'm happy to hear that, Salvador. You're in a position to be a real witness of what Christians should be. And no doubt this office experience will prove to be very valuable for you. By the way, are you going to go with us to the village of San Martin tomorrow? We plan to have a meeting there in the evening."

"Yes, I'm going," the young man replied. "I'm supposed to meet Mayra to practice after vespers tonight. We're preparing a duet for tomorrow at church."

His friendship with Mayra had deepened with the passing months. The trio still spent time practicing, and going with the pastor to sing on his missionary trips. When they returned home at night, Salvador walked the girls back to the dormitory. Amali usually walked on ahead as Salvador and Mayra tended to lag behind, deep in conversation. Their dreams and hopes for the future were their favorite topics. "When I decided to really give my heart to God and be baptized, I began to think I might be a pastor someday," Salvador confided to Mayra. "I know that God saved my life for a purpose. When I finally let Him take the bitterness from my mind, I found hope for my future."

"You'd make an excellent pastor, Salvador." The young girl turned her face toward him. A full moon shone through the trees, and Salvador took her hand as they walked on. He realized then that it really mattered to him what she thought. "Thank you for saying that, Mayra. It's important to me what you think."

He began to count the days till Friday when he'd see Mayra again. He saw an unusual beauty in her now that she was blossoming into a woman. Her features were even and attractive, her olive skin like velvet, her dark eyes warm and sparkling, and her smile infectious. But her outward beauty was not the main attraction. She had a deep and meaningful relationship with God. Like him, she'd suffered the loss of parents. Not only had her father died a brutal death, but her mother had not made an effort to keep in touch. Mayra accepted all this, knowing that God's love for her could fill the void in her heart. And she kept to herself the feelings that stirred her when she was with Salvador. This part of her life was also in God's hands.

Salvador adjusted to his work in the mayor's office, and the general as well as the other office workers learned to respect and trust him. He was given more and more responsibility.

One day when Salvador answered General García's request to come to his office, he saw a well-dressed woman seated there. "I want you to meet my friend, Salvador," the general began, nodding to the woman.

He then turned to Salvador. "This lady is secretary to the vice president of our country."

Salvador greeted her politely, and then the general went on, "Salvador is like a son to me. In fact, I brought him here to the children's home, El Bosque, when he was just a little boy. He had lost all his family in this ugly civil war. But he has graduated with a teacher's certificate, and I brought him here to work because he is one of the most responsible young men that I know. I've often thought that he should be in the military. We need fellows like him in our army."

"I'm very glad to meet you, Salvador," the woman said with a smile. "It is gratifying to meet young people with character and ambition."

Back in his office, Salvador pondered the conversation. *I wonder why people think the army is such a high goal,* he thought. *I plan to be a soldier, all right, but in a different army. If God can use me, I'll be a soldier in His army.*

Salvador was enjoying living on his own and taking care of himself. Once when I was visiting at El Bosque I asked him, "So you're living alone in a house. Who does your cooking?"

"I do," he laughed. "You know, the boys learned to help in the house as well as the girls. I don't mind cooking."

I looked at this handsome, confident young adult. "Have you decided on your lifework?" I asked him. "I think you once told me that you'd like to be a minister."

"Yes, that idea has been in the back of my mind for a long time, actually ever since I was baptized. But I wasn't sure if that was God's plan for me, or even if I could be a minister."

"Listen, son, if God calls you to be a minister, He will help you to do it. The important thing to know is what God's plans are. Pray about it. I'll pray too."

The months rolled by, and Salvador's year of work was almost over. One day in a phone conversation from the ICC office, I asked Juana about Salvador's plans. "I know he has had some interest in taking theology," I told her.

"I haven't talked to him lately, but I think he's still interested."

"Well, discuss it with him because I think I have a sponsor for him, and we need to know."

Later as I discussed different students' plans with the pastor I mentioned that I still hadn't heard from Salvador. "Do you know what he's decided?" I asked. "If he's going back to school this coming year, we need to make plans."

Both the pastor and Juana mentioned it to Salvador, but his mind was in turmoil. Even though he'd cherished the ambition of being a minister since the day he was baptized, he now had second thoughts. He felt overwhelmed by a sense of deep unworthiness. He kept thinking of the years he'd spent filled with a spirit of hate and revenge. He remembered carrying out the orders of guerrilla commanders. He thought of the hand grenades he'd thrown at soldiers. He relived the time he'd helped bring down a helicopter.

With horror, he looked back at the years of violence and agonized, "How can I serve God when I have shed blood?"

Finally one Friday night at Prof Donaldo's home, he couldn't stand it any longer. He had to talk to someone—and there was no one he felt more comfortable with. The teacher and his wife had already retired to their room, but Salvador knocked on their door.

"Can I talk to you?" he asked hesitatingly when they told him to come in.

"Of course, son. What is it?" the teacher answered warmly. "Come and sit on the edge of the bed."

It was hard to know how to start, but there in the darkness Salvador knew that the time had come. Not only did he need to discuss his future, but he'd kept the details of his life story to himself too long. He needed to tell someone about his pain, the lost years of childhood, and the violence. The blood that stained his own hands. God had helped him so much, but it was time to let human friends carry part of his burden. The couple waited expectantly. "Go ahead," Donaldo gently encouraged him. "Say whatever you need to."

So Salvador sat there on the edge of the bed in the shadowed room. A single candle burned on a nearby table. Slowly, softly he began. He told of his happy childhood, then the year of confusion and loneliness when his father was away and they didn't know where he was or if he'd even return. He told of the march to the rebel camp. Of the indoctrination. How he'd been taught to hate and to kill. He told everything—his pain, his guilt, and the choking bitterness he carried throughout his childhood. And now, finally, his fear that he was not worthy to be a minister.

It was into the wee hours of the morning before he finally finished. There were times when he could not go on for the agony of remembering. He put his hands over his face, and tears flowed through his fingers. Donaldo and his wife wept with him.

Finally the tale ended and Salvador cried out, "Don't you see why I'm not worthy to be a minister for God?"

There was a long pause, and Donaldo spoke softly.

"My dear boy, don't you understand that God has forgiven you long ago? Don't you see that He knows you were only a child, the victim of wicked men? He is a God of love. His hand has been over you all this time. He saved you for a purpose. You have a story to tell, a story of God's miraculous deliverance, of a changed heart, and of God's hand in your future. Trust Him, Salvador. Be willing to tell your story so that others can see what God has done for you. I believe that God is calling you to be a minister so that you can be a powerful witness for Him."

Salvador's eyes were swimming with tears. "Do you really mean it, Prof? Can God really use me?"

"I am sure of it, Salvador. But let's pray right now, and then leave it all in God's hands. If He offers you the opportunity, step out in faith and take it."

Back in his room, Salvador looked out his window and saw the stars seemingly hanging like clusters of grapes low in the heavens. His heart was drawn to God in thankfulness and dedication. "Thank You, dear Father in heaven," he prayed. "Thank You for helping me to find the answer. If You will be with me, I'll do whatever You ask."

That night peace came into his heart, and he slept like a child. It was another milestone in his life.

Chapter 28

The next afternoon the school trio went along to a neighboring village to sing for the evangelistic meeting. Sitting with Mayra on the bus as they went homeward, Salvador brought up the subject of his plans for his future. "You know, I've always wanted to be a minister."

"I know," she replied. "And you haven't changed your mind, have you?"

"Not really, but I'll confess I had some second thoughts. But last night I had a long talk with Prof, and the doubts I had have disappeared. What I want to talk to you about, Mayra, is about my plans for college." She looked at him with a question in her eyes. "I didn't know until recently that Mami Fleck has found sponsors for me so that I can go to a Christian college in a neighboring country this coming year to begin my studies."

Her face clouded, and she looked down. "Yes, I always knew you would go there to study, but I guess I didn't realize it would be so soon."

"Have you decided about your own future, Mayra? I know you want to finish your education."

"Yes, I found out that they're going to offer a degree here in home economics. I think I'd like to take that and be a teacher. It will mean four more years."

They rode on in silence, then Salvador spoke again. "You know I care a lot for you, Mayra. If I know my own heart I love you, but I'm wondering what a long separation will do to us."

"I love you too, Salvador, but, like you, I want God's will. What do you think that is?"

"I've given this a lot of thought. I want you to say what you think I should do."

Deep in her heart, Mayra dreaded to think of his leaving for four years of study, but she also knew that she would never stand in his way. "I don't know what the future holds, Salvador," she said, "but I know that I believe you are called to be a minister and that should come first in your life. I think that if you have the opportunity you should go."

Salvador looked into her pretty face. "I'm glad to hear you say that. In one sense I'm thrilled with the opportunity, but I can hardly bear to think of leaving you behind."

He'd never thought seriously of any girl besides Mayra. She seemed to be the perfect one for him in every way. But he knew they must face reality. Before leaving her that evening at the dorm, they agreed to make it a matter of prayer—their feelings for each other and the fact that four years is a long time.

All that week Salvador struggled with the decision, finally deciding to talk with Seño Juana and the Prof the next weekend. He felt surprised when they both gave the same advice: Leave your relationship in God's hands and make your education first.

It was a painful decision, but both young people knew that it was the wise one. They would both pursue their goals and remain friends, but make no promises for the future. That part of their lives they would leave to God's leading.

Word soon came that Salvador should begin preparations to leave for college. There was the application to send, documents to arrange for leaving the country, and, of course, he needed to give notice to the general that he would be leaving.

He found opportunity to talk to General García that week. "I don't know if I have ever shared my goals for the future with you, General," he began.

"No, tell me, what are they?"

Then Salvador explained. "You know, when I came to El Bosque I didn't know anything about God, and for a long time I didn't want to know because of all that had happened to me. But little by little, I began to understand who God really is and what He is like. General, I've learned to know that He is the only answer to life's problems. He has changed my life completely. He died for me, and I am determined to live for Him. I want to be a pastor."

The older man settled back in his chair. "I'm not surprised, Salvador. I know what the people out at El Bosque believe and teach. I haven't let it rub off on me enough, I guess, but I have to say that if there is a true religion, they have it. I've watched you this year, and I respect you and your principles. I would never try to change you."

"General, that isn't all. Of course you know Mami Fleck and what she means to all of us. She's found a sponsor to help me go to college to take theology and prepare to be a minister of the gospel. I've decided to go."

A wry smile came over the general's face. "I might have known that lady would do this to me. I'll have to have some words with her. But, seriously, Salvador, I have supported Mrs. Fleck and all of her group ever since they started here, mostly because I've seen the results of what they are doing. You will make a fine pastor. You can go with my blessing, but it will be a real loss to our office."

"Thank you, General García. You have been a good friend to me, and this year has been a valuable experience. I won't forget it."

The general rose, extending his hand. Salvador rose too, and the older man drew him to him with a back-slapping embrace. "God go with you, son!"

The days of preparation sped by. Salvador spent them in the home of Professor Donaldo and his family. The evening before he was to leave, Salvador saw Mayra one last time. He dreaded the visit, for he knew it would be painful, but there was nothing else to do. The couple tried to keep their conversation upbeat, though their hearts were hurting. "You will write often, won't you, Mayra?" Salvador asked. He knew he'd be lonesome so far from his friends. "Tell me all the news from here, and"—looking into her eyes—"how everything is going with you."

"Of course I'll write, but I'll bet you'll be the one to get too busy! Don't forget you have a good friend back here at El Bosque." There was a wistful look in her eyes, but she tried to stay cheerful too. Finally she looked at her watch. "I have to go back to the dorm, Salvador. I don't want to get into trouble."

"Of course. It's getting late. I'll walk you back." They went into the dining area where Donaldo and his wife were working at the table. Excusing themselves, the two struck off for the half-mile walk to the school. There were long silences as they walked down the path, past the children's homes, and on out through the gate to the main road toward the girls dorm. At times one or the other would make an attempt at conversation, but it was no use. As the lights of the school came closer, their pace slowed. Salvador took her hand. "Mayra, no matter what happens, I'll never forget you. And you can be sure that I will be praying for you."

Mayra, fighting tears, could not speak. At the gate they stopped and stood facing each other. The tropical moon lit their faces.

"Dear Mayra, I pray that God will keep you in His love. I'll look forward to your letters, but I won't hold you to any promises. You can be sure that the memories of our friendship will always be in my heart." Then taking both of her hands he looked down at her. "Let's have one last prayer together."

As he took her in his arms for that final goodbye, their tears flowed, and then she ran for the dorm. He slowly turned away, heading back down the road.

Chapter (29)

On one of my visits to El Bosque before Salvador went away to college, he and I were visiting when I asked if he'd be willing to share his life story with me.

"Of course, Mami Fleck. It is painful for me, but I do want you to know. I want to warn you, though, that it is a long story."

"No problem, son; we'll take all the time we need." We agreed to meet the next afternoon. And so, sitting at the table in my trailer, Salvador told me his story. I'd heard some of the principal parts of the story before, but as he told it from his earliest recollections, I grew more and more amazed.

I was taking notes as fast as I could, but as he quietly told the unbelievable events he'd lived through, I looked up into his face and saw tears in his eyes. I knew he was reliving the pain he'd felt many years before. At times his voice became so very low that I had to ask him to repeat what he'd said. At one point he could only put his head down on his arms and sob, and I could no longer write. We just cried together. That first session lasted four hours. It was a stressful four hours for me, but much more so for him.

When we finally came to the end, it was time for him to leave. I knew that he was going to be leaving the only home that he now knew. Since he'd become an adult, Salvador had formed a closer bond with Ken and me as his parents. Many of the older children began to rely more and more on us for their emotional support and guidance. Just reliving his story with him had sealed that bond, and I knew that Salvador, more than ever, would be my boy. Before going out the door we prayed together, and then he threw his arms around me, and said, "Mami Fleck. I lost my mother, but I found another in you!"

After Salvador left I sat at the table thinking of the story he'd told me. Hundreds of children have come to us through International Children's Care, and every one has a story, a tragedy that brought them to us. But Salvador's story surpassed them all. I knew that as far as Salvador was concerned, there was a missing piece, something that had to be done so he could find closure and be free to go on with his life. He needed to know if his father was alive or dead. I bowed my head there as daylight was fading and the trailer was growing dark. "Lord, look in mercy on this young man, on this boy that You rescued. He has found healing and hope in You, but he needs to know about his father."

The first days at the Adventist university were a maze in Salvador's mind. His life at El Bosque, then at the secondary school, and even in the village working for the general had been rather protected. Although he had been to the capital, he had never lived anyplace else since the day he arrived in the general's helicopter. To be part of a student body of 500 students was a new experience, and at times he wished he were back where everything was familiar to him. El Bosque was *home,* and he sorely missed Prof and his family. Then there was Mayra. At first he wrote frequently, but college life soon consumed his time and interests. After a few months her letters arrived less often, too. Salvador thought of this with some regret, but decided, *It's probably for the best. That phase of my life has to be on hold.*

He was invited to be a member of the college choir, and then he found himself in other singing groups, and often he was asked to sing solos. By his second year he had Greek to tackle. Then there were the extra activities of helping with visitation, Bible studies, and preaching in small churches in the community. Among the student body were friends of his from El Bosque, and they encouraged each other.

An International Children's Care board member saw the need and purchased a house near the university to serve as a home away from home for these students. Several of the boys, including Salvador, lived in the house with a couple who served as house parents. The girls lived in the college dorm, but they all took their meals at the nearby house. I came occasionally to visit. Now that the students were away from their home at El Bosque they relied on me to mother them. I was the one to lend them an ear, to help them with problems, and to see that they had sponsors to pay their expenses.

One day in the capital, on my way to El Bosque, I happened to pick up a newspaper. An article jumped out at me. It told that many of the civil war refugees had come back into their villages and received amnesty by the new government. I thought, *Could it be possible that Salvador's father might show up? He has always wondered if his father is dead or alive. Maybe he should go back to his village to investigate.*

While at El Bosque I discussed the possibility with Prof Donaldo and Juana. "I just feel that we need to make it possible for Salvador to go back to his village and find out if he has any family left, especially if his father is alive."

"I would be willing to go with him, Mrs. Fleck, if you would want me to," Donaldo offered.

"Let's see if we can arrange it," I suggested. "If he goes, someone should go with him, and you are the logical person. I'll tell you what let's do: I'm going on to the university on this trip. Salvador has two weeks' vacation coming up, and this might be the right time for you to go. I'll talk to him and let you know."

When I suggested the plan to Salvador he jumped at the idea. "Would you really do this, Mami Fleck? There is nothing I want more than to find out if my father still lives."

"I've already talked to Prof Donaldo, and he is willing to go with you. If you can get away, let's do it this next week. We'll get you a plane ticket." Noting the look of concern in his face, I added, "Don't worry, Salvador, this will be my gift to you. Donaldo will meet you in the capital and go with you up to the high country and your old home."

"Really, Mami Fleck?"

The excitement in his face was ample assurance that this was the right thing to do. Soon the arrangements were made. Salvador would arrive at the capital by plane, Donaldo would take a night bus so that he would be there to meet him, and they would leave that same day for the long trip to his village.

On the morning that I was leaving, the students in our house at the university were gathered for morning worship. I told them, "Salvador will soon be leaving on a very important mission. Let's pray today that his trip will be successful and that God will help him find the information he needs." We prayed that God's special blessing would attend this young man who needed to find the missing pieces of his life.

Later, at the airport, Salvador was there to help me with my luggage. I turned to tell him goodbye. "I believe that God has something special in mind for your life, Salvador. I can't promise what you will find on this trip back to your old home, but I know your faith and commitment to God are strong. This trip will be an emotional experience for you, but I know you can handle it. I will be praying for you, and you can be sure that I love you as one of my own sons."

Chapter 30

Salvador arrived at the City Center on and found Donaldo waiting for him. The City Center had grown into a well-staffed, well-equipped temporary shelter for abandoned children. María Feldmann, who had helped me at the very beginning of this program for children, was now the director of the receiving center. It also served as a central office where more resources were available.

María called me by telephone. "Salvador and Donaldo are here, and they'll be leaving on an early bus for the highlands."

"Wonderful!" I replied. "Be sure that Salvador calls me when they return. I'll be so anxious to know what happens and if he learns anything about his father."

Bright and early the next morning the two were on their way. Salvador had mixed emotions—elation at the thought of possibly hearing news of his father and apprehension, fearing bad news. The crowded bus headed west toward the high country on the first leg of their journey to the isolated village. He sat looking out the window, deep in thought. Finally, he turned to his friend. "You know, Prof, it is strange. This is something I wanted and really had to do, but now I'm not sure about it. I guess I'm scared."

"That's understandable, son. This is bringing back a lot of painful memories and, of course, you don't know what you will find."

"Yes, it really is strange. In a way I'm afraid we won't learn anything and the trip will be for nothing. On the other hand, I'm afraid of what we may run into."

"There is probably some of the old fear of the army hanging over you, too, isn't there?"

"Maybe. Anyway, I'm glad you're with me," Salvador said, turning to this man who had proved to be almost a father, and a true friend.

"Well, we're in this together," the teacher said with a reassuring smile.

Late that evening they arrived at the last town of any size. Donaldo had arranged for them to stay with a friend's family. They'd start out early the next morning for Salvador's village. By now they were in the highlands, known as Indian country. Most of its population were descended from the ancient Mayan civilization and still held to many of their old customs. The majority of the village's houses were of adobe with handmade, red tiled roofs. The streets in the center of town were paved with cobblestones, and a large old Spanish colonial church faced the central park. Donaldo soon found the home of his friends.

"Bienvenidos!" ("Welcome!") their host greeted them, opening the door wide. *"Pase adelante!"* ("Come right in!")

The two travelers were glad to see that they'd arrived

just in time for the evening meal. Donaldo was soon talking with the family, but Salvador was quiet, his thoughts preoccupied with the object of the trip. But soon the conversation turned to Salvador's return to his home.

"You'll have to go to Central Park to wait for a bus up into the mountains," the host explained. "And I'm not sure you can get all the way to your village. Since that is a mountain road and off the main track, I doubt that many buses go there. You may have to catch a ride on a truck or walk the last leg of your journey."

"Have you heard of any unrest in this area?" Donaldo asked. "I know that there's still been some terrorist activity at times."

"I don't think you'll have any problems," the man replied. "It's been quite a while since there have been reports of any violence in this area."

"We'll put our trust in God," Salvador said.

The two waited most of the morning for the right bus to come along. When one finally arrived it was already loaded with men, women, and children—most in the typical dress of their particular villages. Along with the human cargo, the bus held baskets of produce (most of it stashed on top of the bus) as well as huge baskets of chickens and even some little piglets tied together. The seats were already full, so they stood in the swaying bus until a seat was vacated. It was a long trip, since the bus stopped every few minutes to let someone off or someone else on. Finally, late in the afternoon, they climbed off the bus at the last village on the mountain road before Salvador's home village. This was the end of the bus route.

Salvador felt a tremor of excitement. "I remember

where we are now," he told Donaldo as they got off the bus. "It's about an hour and a half walk from here. If some vehicle doesn't come along to give us a ride, we'll have to walk." And that's what they did. They grabbed their bags and started out. They were clearly getting into the mountains. Finally, after a long climb, they crested the hill and stopped. A beautiful valley spread out down below them, and they saw a village in the distance. Smoke curled up from some of the red tile-roofed homes. The spire of the village church lifted high above surrounding trees. Breathless, Salvador cried, "Prof! There it is! That is my village!"

His heart was pounding, and deep emotions flooded his mind. After 16 years, he was about to go home. But it wouldn't really be home, for no family waited there to welcome him. If he could just get some word about his father. What would the next few hours bring?

Salvador urged Donaldo to hurry as they neared the edge of the village. "Come, Prof! I know the way to my house!" Then he stopped short. "But it probably isn't there anymore. Many of the houses were bombed and burned."

"Well, we'll soon find out," Donaldo said. He sensed the inevitable tension and anxiety in Salvador. *This is going to be the most emotional experience I can imagine,* he thought as they began the last few steps toward the town. *I just pray that the news will be good. Salvador has overcome so much, I don't know how much more he can take.*

Rounding a corner, Salvador stopped short. "There it is!" Then coming closer to the house, he cried, "It looks the same! Can it really be true?"

"It looks like someone lives there," Prof told him.

"Who could it be?" Salvador thought aloud. "My family are dead, at least my mother is. It wouldn't be possible that my father is there."

"No, probably not. The house likely has new owners by now." Donaldo didn't want him to have false hopes.

"Let's go next door," Salvador suggested. "They can tell us who lives there." Without some preparation, he wasn't ready to face what he'd find in his old home.

They knocked on the door, and the woman who answered seemed wary of their questions. She didn't speak much Spanish, but they finally made her understand. She was reluctant to reply. Why did they want to know who lived next door? In a village that had suffered the ravages of a civil war, people were not quick to give out information. But finally she pointed to the house and said two words, "Magdalena Escobar."

Magdalena! *No, it's impossible!*

"Impossible!" he spoke aloud. "Magdalena was my mother's name. But she's dead, so it can't be her. And anyway, her name isn't Escobar." The color drained from Salvador's face. He swallowed once. And again. He was trying to regain composure. His heart was pounding. *Oh, God! Help me! Please be with me right now.*

The neighbor closed her door, and the two men walked on toward the other house. Salvador was trembling. They stopped a little distance away from it.

"Prof, could it be possible that someone with the name Magdalena just happens to live there? It can't be my mother!"

"Tell me, Salvador. Did anyone else in your family have the same name as your mother?"

Salvador looked down at the ground, searching his memory. But a jumble of thoughts tumbled through his mind. He wasn't sure his mind was even functioning at that point. Then he looked up. "You know, I remember now that my mother had a sister with the same first name, but we called her *Tia* Ana" [Aunt Ana].

"Well, maybe she lives there now," Donaldo said, glad for this possibility. "At least if she does we can probably get some information."

So they stepped up to the house and knocked. A woman came to the door. At the sight of her, Salvador went weak and thought he would faint. This was not his Aunt Ana! It looked like his mother, but it couldn't be!

Yet though this woman was older, her face lined with age, her resemblance to his memory of his mother turned him cold. He stood as if transfixed! It had been so long. Was the picture he'd kept in his mind of his mother dependable? Time seemed to stand still. He remembered that the neighbor had given him a last name different from his family name. But what a resemblance. He couldn't take his eyes from her face.

The woman stood there, her expression puzzled. Who were these men? What did they want? She waited for one of them to speak.

Salvador finally found his voice. "Do you mind telling me your name?" he asked softly. Then he realized that she didn't speak much Spanish and had not understood him. He asked again, more slowly, *"Como se llama?"*

She hesitated. She had learned to be wary of

strangers. But she looked at Salvador with a quizzical expression. Then she made her decision. With hesitation she spoke: "Magdalena de Escobar." She seemed confused, however, and turned away to call someone else in the house.

Salvador looked at Donaldo, desperation in his eyes. "I don't know what to think! Prof, this isn't my aunt! She . . . she looks like my mother. But she can't be. My mother is dead!"

Donaldo was at a loss for words. Who could know what the next moment would bring? "I'm praying for you, Salvador," he said. "Just be calm. There must be some answer."

When the woman returned, a girl was with her.

"My mother doesn't speak Spanish well. Can I help you?" she asked. It was obvious that the girl's Spanish was limited, too.

Aside, Salvador whispered to Donaldo, "I've forgotten the dialect, but maybe I can make out some words." Then turning to the woman, he asked again, "Your name. What is your name?"

The girl answered, "Her name is Magdalena de Escobar."

Salvador tried another tack. "Have you lived here long?"

Each question was repeated to the woman in her dialect and then answered in her dialect. The girl then repeated the answer in her faltering Spanish. "*Si, muchos años.*" ("Yes, many years.")

His breath ragged, Salvador ventured again, "Did you go through a hard time in the civil war?"

As the question was translated, the woman's face clouded, but she finally answered cautiously, "Yes, we all did."

He pressed on, now unable to wait, yet fearing the answer. "Did you ever live in a camp up in the mountains?"

She nodded. Both she and the girl looked startled. *How did this man know so much?*

By then Salvador had noticed a birthmark on the woman's neck, and suddenly he remembered a triangular birthmark on his own mother's neck. He looked closer. It was the same! A conviction was gripping him. *Could this possibly be?* But he had to know more!

The woman's face had grown pale. Salvador continued to question her. "Did you have another husband before this one?"

When she seemed unable to speak, but slowly nodded, he realized that this must be his mother. He was afraid to believe it. He had but one more question. "Did you have a husband by the name of Manuel Gomez?"

The expression on the woman's face was tense. She was afraid. *Who could this be?* "Yes," she answered. "But how could you know?"

"Did you have a son by that husband?" Salvador pressed.

The woman crumpled and began to weep. "Oh yes! My only son, and they took him away and killed him. I lost my only son!" And she wept bitterly. The girl, who appeared to be her daughter, began to comfort her, speaking the strange dialect in a soft endearing tone.

It is my mother! It really is my mother! Tears pushed against his eyelids, and Salvador struggled to keep control. How could he break the news to her?

At last he could stand no more. He wondered if he were dreaming again. But no, Donaldo was there with him. He was standing in front of his mother! He wanted desperately to throw himself into her arms, but he knew he had to wait. He had to prepare her.

Praying earnestly for strength and help, he asked her ever so gently, "Was that son's name Oscar?"

Both mother and daughter stared at him in astonishment, disbelief in their eyes. *Who is this man?* The older woman looked into his eyes, long and hard. There was something familiar about him.

Tears streamed down his face as he cried out in the best dialect he could muster, "Mama, I am that son. I am Oscar!"

Her tears suddenly turned to astonishment. She grabbed him and began to jump and dance, screaming and shouting, "My son! My lost boy!"

That next moment will live forever in the memory of that lost boy. He was enfolded in his mother's arms, and her cries of joy brought all the neighbors running. His tears and hers flowed together. He hardly comprehended that his mother could be *here in his arms*. Was it a dream? She had been killed! For now, all he knew was that God had brought an answer that he never expected in this life. He thought his heart would burst.

They stood wrapped in each other's arms while the daughter looked on, her eyes wide with wonder. Donaldo, who had been standing by, speechless, realized that he too was weeping. He had come to help Salvador with whatever happened, but at that moment he felt weak and dizzy. His own emotions had reached a pitch that was beyond words.

Finally, with one arm still around Salvador, Magdalena turned to the girl. "Ana, this is your brother! This is Oscar! The one we thought was dead!"

When the full realization of the truth dawned on her, the girl began to jump up and down too, hugging Salvador, and crying. "Oh, *papi*, you are my long-lost brother. Oh! I love you!" (In that culture, *papi* is an affectionate name for any close male family member.)

With all the screaming and crying, neighbors were coming. Whatever was happening at Magdalena's house?

Soon people began to gather. Salvador still could not believe how it could be, but the explanations would come later. They went into the house—the same house where he'd lived as a child. The house that had belonged to his grandparents. All his mother could say was, "God is so good. He saved my life, and now I know that He saved my boy, too!"

Ana looked up at Salvador. "Mama has talked about you so much," she said, hugging him again.

Soon the house was full of people, and Salvador found that five of his sisters still lived. Ana was the baby that had been born up at the guerrilla camp, the little sister that he scarcely knew.

There was never a more exciting homecoming, nor one so filled with emotion, tears and joy. There would be sad things to remember and explain, but that would come later. For this night there was only pure happiness.

Chapter (31)

As he entered the house, Salvador turned to his mother and sister. "I want you to meet Professor Donaldo López. He is not only a dear friend, but he has been like a father to me."

Magdalena turned grateful eyes to Donaldo. "May God bless you and reward you for what you have done for my son," she told him. Between Salvador and Ana, they translated her message—a mixture of Spanish and her native dialect.

The news of Salvador's arrival spread fast. Neighbors hurried in from different directions. Soon other family members began to arrive. Salvador didn't recognize his older sister, Ana, when she came with her husband. Magdalena was almost too excited to talk, but grabbing the young woman by the arm, she kept saying, "Ana! Ana!" At first he was confused. She had just introduced the young girl as Ana, his little sister. Then he remembered that the youngest child, born at the guerrilla camp, was given the same name as her older sister. Ana threw her arms around him, crying, "My little brother! Is it really you? Are you really alive?"

Wiping the tears from his eyes, Salvador turned to Donaldo. "This is my oldest sister. I can't believe she is still alive! She was very involved in the civil war with the guerrillas." Then noticing Donaldo's puzzled look at meeting another Ana, he hurriedly explained, "I remember that my mother worried about Ana's dangerous role with the guerrillas. She feared her daughter would be killed, and the name Ana, taken from my grandmother, must stay in the family." And Donaldo began to comprehend some of the family's trauma during the years spent at the guerrilla camp.

Soon another young woman stepped up. "Son," his mother cried excitedly, "this is Margarita!" Salvador stared at the young woman. "But I thought you were dead!" He remembered seeing his sister Teresita led into the house of murder. He had always thought she was the last of his immediate family, except his father. There were more hugs and more tears.

He had just recuperated from the shock of seeing Margarita, when another young woman crowded up to the circle. "Here is your other sister, Oscar! This is Magdalena!" Salvador stared wide-eyed at this seeming stranger, but he was soon smothered in her arms as she cried, "Oscar! Oscar! Where did you come from!" Again Donaldo was puzzled with the duplication of names. He soon learned that names were important to pass down the heritage of family. She was named after her mother."

The house was filling up. Magdalena's family all lived in the village or close by. There were aunts and uncles, cousins, his sister's husbands and children. Only his father's family had joined the guerrilla band. There was a hubbub of exclamations, everyone asking questions. Salvador felt his head swimming. He wondered, *Am I really awake or is this another dream!* His mother clung to him, never leaving his side. Little Ana, too, kept close, looking up into his face with adoring eyes.

Someone came in with chairs and benches. The curious neighbors began to drift away, and Salvador and Donaldo sat in the midst of the closest family and a few of Magdalena's best friends. There were so many unanswered questions. But more than anything else Salvador was anxious to hear about his father. He felt sure by now that there was no hope of finding him alive. After all, his mother now had another last name. She must be remarried.

With the help of her daughters, Magdalena began to recount the story. When she would be overcome with emotion and break into tears, one of her daughters would continue.

"After the alarm at the big camp, our whole family relocated near one of the cabins on our ranch. When the helicopters began to circle our family camp, we knew they would soon be bombing, and your father told us, 'Every one look out for yourself. Don't worry about anyone else.' I had Baby Ana and wrapped her in the shawl on my back and took Rosita by the hand. I ran for the mountains. I didn't have time to look for the other girls, but just hoped that someone else did. Soon I could look back and see six helicopters strafing the camp. I hoped and prayed that everyone escaped. For nine days we stayed hidden in the mountains. I found a stream for water, but had only a little food that I had grabbed up as I went." Magdalena stopped talking and buried her face in her hands, weeping. When she could collect herself, she went on.

"It was hard. I could nurse the baby, but I didn't have enough food for Rosita and me. After nine days I finally ventured to walk to the village. My mother's house was still vacant, so we came here, hoping that the soldiers would not come and bother us.

"I didn't know what had happened to the rest of you. News finally came to the village about the massacre, and I was afraid that you had all been killed. The story that came was too terrible to believe." Magdalena could not go on. Reliving that horrible drama convulsed her into sobs. Salvador wept as she talked.

Then Margarita took up the tale. "Two months later my sister Magdalena and I came walking into the house. Our father had found us. We stayed with Papi in the mountains until he felt it was safe enough to send us home. He brought us close enough so we could come the rest of the way by ourselves, but he didn't come back for two years."

By then Magdalena was drying her eyes and could continue the story. "When he did come home, he told me all he knew—how you had come during the massacre. He knew you had been put in the line along with Teresita and all the rest of our family. He had been rounded up with the rest of those who were killed, but right after you got there he was able to escape.

"Four days later when the soldiers all left and no one was around he went to the camp and looked in the house where they had put the bodies. He found Teresita, but couldn't find any of the rest of our immediate family. I told him then what I had found out. One of your uncles had seen you in an army car in the village. Then someone else saw the big white helicopter come, and they saw them put you in it. We knew then that they had taken you away to kill you, too." She could not go on.

Her daughter continued the story. "Father was here with us for a little while. We were all mourning for you, Teresita, and our older brothers, but we hoped that the troubles were over and that Papa could stay with us. Of course, he still went out to his farm, trying to put it all back together. But one evening a group of men came to the door, calling Papa outside. Soon he came back in, telling us that these men said they needed him to go with them to sign some papers. But he told Mama, 'I'm sure it is only a pretext. I think they have me at last, and I can't run anymore. I am endangering the rest of you.'"

As Magdalena told the rest of the story, they all wept together. "He told us all goodbye. He knew he would not be coming back. I'll never forget that moment. Mama was crying and clinging to him, and he was crying too. He said, 'I'm sorry, Maggie, for what I have done to you and all the family. If I had only known what we were getting into. Please forgive me. I love you.'

"We never saw him again. They took him to the river and killed him there. Our uncle found his body later."

Donaldo had sat spellbound, listening to the revelation. Now he looked at Salvador anxiously, knowing that this final news would quell his hopes of finding his father alive. He silently prayed, *Lord, comfort and sustain him. We need You right now.*

200

At that moment Salvador felt that he could finally mourn for his father. The pain in his heart and the disappointment of knowing that he could never find him alive were intense. But there was a finality. The insecurity—the feeling that he must go and search—all of it died then. His feelings were a mixture of the bitter and the sweet. He finally knew his father was dead, but some of his immediate family were alive! He felt a sort of peace, mixed with the joy of knowing that his mother and sisters still lived and were right there with him.

Suddenly the story was interrupted by a sound at the door, and a man Salvador didn't know came in. His mother arose to meet him and then drew him into the circle. "José, this is my son, Oscar. This is the boy that we thought was dead, but he is alive! Oscar, this is your stepfather."

The man stepped forward and wrapped Salvador in his arms. "My boy! Oh, what wonderful news! You are alive. We have mourned so long for you. Now you will be my son." And José wept as he held this young man whom he would now accept as a son.

Then Salvador motioned to Donaldo. "I want you to meet my friend, Donaldo," he told his stepfather. "He is a very dear friend." The man greeted Donaldo warmly, and they all found seats again.

As José joined the family group, the oldest girl began to explain. "Oscar, you need to know what kind of a man José is. He was a friend of our father, of our whole family. For five years he watched the suffering of our family, and he saw how our mother was struggling to care for us alone. He did what he could to help. But finally he asked my mother to let him marry her and take care of us all and be a father and protector, and that is what he has done. We couldn't love him more if he were our real father."

Then José spoke up. "It is true. I couldn't bear to see what your mother was going through, trying to raise these little girls alone. I knew that if I married her I would need to think of these daughters as my own, and that is what I have done."

There was an immediate bond between Salvador and this man, and in his heart he thanked God for sending that kind of a man to his family. He accepted him whole-heartedly, feeling the depth of José's love and kindness.

There were other stories to tell. Ana, the oldest girl, told what had happened to her. Salvador was surprised that she had survived, because he knew that she'd been highly trained in the guerrilla movement and had been made the commander over a youth group. But she was apparently of the same metal as Salvador. She was captured by the military and marched into the mountains in a similar way as her brother was. Her captors used every means they knew to force her to give information. Her arms were tied behind her, and she was made to keep up with the soldiers. After days of marching they passed by a deep ravine with trees and brush at the bottom. Suddenly Ana threw herself over the edge. Thinking she had probably killed herself, the commander ordered the men to keep going and not try to find her. Eventually she found her way back home.

Before they realized it, someone reminded them that it was 10:30, way past their regular bedtime. Margarita, who lived across the street, put her arm around her brother. "Come and stay with us," she said. "We have room." She knew her mother didn't have extra beds.

Her husband also urged, "Yes, we have plenty of room."

But Salvador felt so emotionally drained that he needed a little time to absorb what had happened. Donaldo was relieved to hear his reply. "We've already reserved a room at the little *pensión* here in the village. We'll stay there tonight and tomorrow night with you."

Donaldo, too, needed some time to absorb all he'd witnessed. His own emotions were at the breaking point. He thought, *This is all incredible. I can't imagine how Salvador has held up as well as he has.*

Magdalena had told Salvador about his other sister, Rosita, who lived with her family a few miles from the village. Before leaving, they heard José announce, "I'm going out to Rosita's place to let her know that her brother is here." When Salvador heard that it was a walk of an hour and a half, he realized how true it was what they had said about this man.

As Salvador and Donaldo walked down the cobblestone road to their *pensión* their hearts were so full they could hardly contain the emotion. At last Salvador tried to put some of his wonder into words. "Prof, I've never been so sure that God lives, that He is real, and that He is interested in every one of us. Can you believe how God was intervening in my life and that of my family even before I had accepted Him? And I so much appreciate your coming with me, that I didn't have to meet this alone."

"Son, I was praying for you all evening. I don't know how you stood up so well, except for God's help. It was almost more than I could handle, I must confess."

It had been a long day—so much had happened. As Salvador lay down on his cot that night, his heart was filled with thanksgiving, with happiness. "I'll remember this day as long as I live," he told his friend.

Chapter 32

*T*he village was astir early, and in the *pensión* where Salvador and Donaldo stayed they woke to the usual sounds of village life. Roosters were crowing. The *clip-clopping* of horses sounded on the cobblestone street outside their window. A baby cried nearby. Kettles were banging in the kitchen of the *pensión,* and there was the pungent smell of wood fires. It all brought Salvador to the realization that he was back in his home village. The *slap-slap* of the maid making tortillas reminded him that he was hungry and that they were going to his mother's house for breakfast. When he first awoke he rubbed his eyes to be sure he was awake and not dreaming, a dream that was too good to be true.

Looking across at Donaldo's bed, he saw that his friend was stirring. "How did you sleep, Prof?" he asked.

"Well, I have to admit it took me awhile to get to sleep. I don't know how you handled all that happened yesterday, Salvador. I have never been in such an emotional situation before. My stomach was in knots. In fact, it still is. I think I'll have to take something before I can eat."

"I'm sorry, Prof. I'll ask my mother to make you one of her teas. I know that you were feeling for me. I'm surprised that I went right to sleep. Somehow, in spite of everything, a load seemed to be lifted from my heart yesterday. I just have such a sweet sense of God's presence. I guess I knew down deep that my father was dead, and it is a relief to be rid of the uncertainty, to finally know everything there is to know about my family. I am so happy that I still have some family and that they care so much about me."

"I am really happy for you, Salvador, and I, too, feel sure that God has had a hand in everything. I guess we had better be getting ready. I imagine your mother has been up for some time preparing breakfast for her long-lost son."

As they neared the house, they realized that the activities of the day were in full swing. Children were in the yard—Salvador's nieces and nephews—and came running to meet them. "Uncle Oscar!" they cried as they raced to see which ones could grab his hands first. "Grandma has breakfast all ready."

Her daughters were there helping her, and the kitchen was the center of bustling activities. When Magdalena saw him she rushed to meet him with a big hug. *"Buenos dias, mi hijo querido,"* she said, giving him an extra squeeze. ("Good morning, my dear son.")

"Buenos dias, mamá," Salvador replied.

Just then a young woman rushed up to him. "Oscar! Do you know me?"

"This is your sister, Rosita," his mother told him. "She came to town early to see you."

Oscar wrapped his sister in his arms, then pushed her back to look at her. "Rosita! Is it really you?" Then he hugged her again. There were tears in everyone's eyes. "I thought you were all dead!" he told her. "I never expected to see you again."

"And we never expected to see you!" she replied. "This is the best surprise of my life!"

Rosita was just a toddler when the tragedy struck. She couldn't remember her big brother, but she had heard all about him and had shared in the grief with her mother of losing this only son.

Breakfast was a joyous occasion. They had ranch-style eggs along with refried beans, bread, milk, tortillas, and corn coffee. Salvador and Donaldo were served first as the honored guests, and seated with his mother, his sisters and their husbands. The children were all fed later.

"This will be a day of fiesta," the older sister told the guests." Mama has sent word to all our family and friends to come and spend the day with us. We want them to see Oscar and share in our joy."

And sure enough, the breakfast was no sooner cleared away than people began to arrive, each one bringing something to contribute to the feast. The kitchen was a separate room at the back of the house. The fire burned briskly in the built-in woodstove. Already huge pots of food were cooking. The women were all dressed in the typical handwoven skirts and embroidered blouses in the colors of that village. Their skirts were long lengths of red handwoven material. The weaving was done in such a way that when they wound the skirt around them there were white stripes down the sides and at the bottom. Each woman and girl wore a beautiful blouse made of handwoven material, and then intricately embroidered in flowered designs of many colors.

The men stood around outside, all talking to Salvador and Donaldo. As the different family members arrived, Salvador was presented to them. Some of them he remembered from his childhood, and all of them had heard of this son who was thought to be dead.

Almost everyone in that village had lost family members in the civil war. Many of those who came that day told Salvador of a child that had been lost and feared dead. His mother's cousin and husband arrived with their two daughters. "Do you remember your aunt Margarita?" his mother asked him. He remembered that his sister Margarita was named after this aunt.

"Yes, of course. I'm so glad to see you again," Salvador greeted them both as they embraced him.

As soon as the opportunity came, the uncle asked Salvador, "Did you, by any chance, ever hear about a little girl that was lost? On the day of the bombing there was so much confusion, everyone running in different directions. Margarita had the baby in her arms, and I grabbed the next youngest. We thought that Ana was right behind us. She was only 2 years old, but walking. But then when we looked around she wasn't there. We could never find her. We don't know if she is dead or alive." This little Ana was also named after the maternal grandmother.

Salvador thought for a moment. Could it be possible? He remembered Ruthie, the little girl that was sick and came on the same helicopter as he did to El Bosque. Yes, he knew she was his cousin, and she had to be Margarita's lost child. He looked at these parents and saw the deep pain and anxiety in their eyes. "Your little girl is alive! I know where she is!"

"Really! Are you sure?" Margarita began to cry.

Her husband quickly spoke up. "Tell us! What do you know?"

"She was at the same orphanage where I was, and she was adopted by an American family. I have heard about her recently. She is in a Christian home with people who love her."

Margarita began to jump up and down, shouting and screaming, "My little girl is alive!"

As people crowded around, Salvador told the family all he knew about Ruthie, how she had been brought in the same helicopter with him. They both thought that their parents were dead.

The mother was beside herself, crying and laughing all at once. But a little later she began to think about her little lost girl and where she is now. "Thank God, she is alive. I am so glad that she was placed with Christian people who took care of her, and I am so glad that a good family loves her and treats her as their own child. But I wish we could see her. She must be a young lady now."

"If you want to write her a letter I'm sure I can get it to her." Salvador remembered that Ruthie had recently written him a letter. Soon there were other families surrounding him. "We lost a child too. Were there more children that you heard of?"

Sadly, Salvador had no good news for anyone else.

Listening in, Donaldo thought, *This place was in the very center of the conflict and the atrocities of the worst of the war! I have never seen such widespread grief!*

By late afternoon the celebration was in full swing. There was lots of food. A huge kettle of tamales was brought out, the typical kind, cooked in banana leaves for special occasions. There were the other tamales, ground corn, wrapped in corn husks. There were different breads and crackers, and a typical cornbread, more like corn cake. Salvador enjoyed the atol, a sweet, hot, thick drink made of finely ground corn and rice and laced with cinnamon sticks. The entertainment consisted of food and visiting. Inevitably, the conversation often turned to the dark days of the civil war and the massacre. Nearly every family had lost someone.

Although everyone had something to tell, the main focus was on Salvador. Everyone strained to hear his every word. Late in the day he began to tell his story to an attentive audience. There were interruptions of questions. First he told of his days up on the mountain when he was left alone in the camp. When he came to the scene at the house and the massacre, sobbing could be heard around the room, and he himself had a hard time continuing. He described the march with the army, the threats, the pain, the grief, and then finally, when he was sure they would kill him in the cell. There were gasps and murmurings of horror. When he came to the part about Captain Salvador and his new name, his little sister interrupted. "I was wondering why Señor Donaldo calls you Salvador." Salvador smiled and said, "That is the reason, but you can call me Oscar if you would rather." Then he recounted all that had happened in his life since leaving the barracks in the helicopter.

"I suffered a lot, especially the first few years, because I thought my family was all dead, all except my father. I knew he had escaped from the lineup, but I thought that if he still lived, he would look for a way to find me. But in looking back, I know now that God had His hand over me, and brought something good out of that tragedy.

"The place where they took me is called El Bosque. It is a long ways from here, not in the mountains like here, but in a jungle. But it is built in what is like a big pine forest. Houses have been made so that 10 or 12 children live in each home with a married couple, who become their parents. It was like a family. These are Christian people who treat the children with love, and teach them about a God of love. They taught us to read and understand the Bible, to learn about God's plan for us, His commandments. And especially how He sent His Son, Jesus, to come down here to our world to show us how to live, and then to die for us. The best thing we learned is that Jesus went back to heaven to prepare homes for us, and soon He is coming back to get us."

Then he turned toward Donaldo. "This man was like a second father to me. He was a father in the home where I lived. Then he became a teacher. It was people like him who taught me about God."

José spoke up. "We all want to thank you, sir, for what you have done for our son, and all the other children."

Donaldo smiled at them through tears. He was feeling the emotion that he knew Salvador was experiencing. He would never forget it.

Someone asked Salvador the question "How could they feed so many children?"

"Well, it is sponsored by an organization in the United States that helps children in many parts of the world. It is called International Children's Care. The director from there is a woman that we all call Mami Fleck. Her husband is Papi Fleck. They were the ones that came and helped to start the program. When I first went, there were only three or four houses, but now there are 11, and they are planning to build more. There are still many children who need homes and care. Actually, I happen to have a picture with me that was taken of me with Papi Fleck." He brought the picture from his pocket, and everyone crowded around to see it.

His mother was deeply moved and said, "Oh! I wish I could see these people to thank them for what they did for you. I am so glad that God sent Christian people to care for you."

Then Salvador went on. "The people at El Bosque believe in giving all the children an education to prepare them, not only for heaven, but for this life too. There is a primary school, in which all the children get the first six grades, and then there is a secondary school, in which they can begin to study for careers. I became a teacher. But besides that, they teach many other things. I worked in the carpentry shop, and I can now get a job anyplace as a carpenter. The girls all learn a lot about how to be good wives and mothers, besides other careers.

"I thought I might be a teacher, but when I learned

what it really means to know God, I knew I wanted to be a pastor. So that is what I am doing now. I am studying at a Christian university. I have two more years before I will be a pastor."

As his mother listened, her heart swelled with pride and happiness. *My son will be a pastor.*

Chapter (33)

*L*ater in the afternoon, Salvador wanted to walk down through the village to see if it was as he remembered. The rest of the family agreed to go with him, as well as friends who'd come for the celebration. By the time they started down the rough stone road toward the center of the village, a crowd had joined them. Word went around quickly. Donaldo and Salvador—his mother and José beside him on one side, his sisters on the other—were surrounded by neighbors, friends, and even some curious onlookers. They headed what looked like a parade. Afterward Donaldo told Mami Fleck, "They treated him like he was the pope!"

As afternoon shadows lengthened, the guests began to leave for their homes. Each one gave Salvador a warm embrace and wished him Godspeed. Soon only the close family members remained. Evening candles were lit, giving a soft glow to the room. Magdalena's heart overflowed with joy. José was with her, thrilled with the happiness that these past two days had brought to his wife. His love for her was deep and unselfish. This long-lost son would be precious to him, too. He was anxious to re-store as much of a family life as possible to Magdalena.

"There has been a lot of tragedy in our lives," Magdalena told Salvador the next day. "I missed all those years of your growing up. But I believe that God has had His hand over you. I never could have done all of this for you."

"Yes, Mamá, I, too, believe that God had His hand over us all the time and turned it all out for good."

"Mi querido hijo" ("My dear son"), she went on, "you said that you must go back to the university and finish your studies. I can hardly bear to think of your leaving us again so soon. Please promise me that you will come back."

"I promise, Mamá. I will never forget that this is my home, and I will come back as often as I can. And I will write to you."

"There is something else, son," she continued. "Little Ana has been able to have only three grades of school. She is begging me to let her go with you. She wants to study like you have. She is 16, and you know that in our village most girls marry by this age."

"I know," he answered. "I've been thinking about this, and I have an idea. I haven't yet told you that Mami Fleck is the one who arranged for me to come and see if I could find my family. She is a second mother to me, and I know she would try to help us with Ana. I'll be talking to her soon by telephone, and we'll see what can be done."

"Ana is the only child I have left at home," his mother went on. "But I would trust you with deciding what is best. And I would trust these people who have done so much for you."

The day went by too soon. That evening they all gathered at Magdalena's house again. The fire was set in the open hearth, the leftover dinner warmed up, and Salvador enjoyed once more the comfort food he had remembered so many times. There was still so much to talk about. Salvador wanted to know more of what had happened during the years that had passed, and his family had many questions about his life at El Bosque.

"I wish you could all go there and visit," he told them. "It is like a refuge out there in the jungle. They provided homes for us, and we never lacked for food or clothing. I know now that God really held His hand over me during those years, and I plan to use my life in serving Him."

Salvador was surprised at his mother's reply. "During those hard years we learned to know about God, too. He is the one who sustained us through all the suffering and hardships, and now I know He is the one who brought you back to us." She wiped the tears from her eyes. "If you are going to be a pastor, you must teach us all that you know, too."

"I have to go back to the university now, Mamá, but I'll be back when I can stay longer. Maybe I can relearn to talk in our dialect again!" They all laughed at that. It had been so strange to have to talk to his mother through a translator.

As the hour grew late, Salvador's brother-in-law—Margarita's husband—suggested, "We have prepared beds for you at our house across the street. I'm sure you are tired and must travel again tomorrow. When you are ready we can go."

"Yes, it has been a big day for all of us," Salvador agreed. "We'll see you again in the morning before we leave, Mamá," he said, putting his arms around her. "I'm so happy I've found you!"

"You can't be any happier than I am, son. If I had to die tonight, I would die happy! But we will expect you here for breakfast in the morning. Good night. We all love you so much." And Magdalena wrapped her arms around him again, kissing his cheek, and then patted his face with both hands.

Salvador and Donaldo were both emotionally spent, but happy. Salvador dropped off to sleep with a happiness in his heart beyond description.

Chapter (34)

At the crack of dawn Salvador and Donaldo were up and preparing for their trip back to the city. Their breakfast was ready, with Magdalena and her daughters doing all they could to give them a good send-off. Salvador realized that even though the typical food that his mother cooked was simple, it was *comfort food* to him, bringing back his days of childhood. It was hard to say goodbye so soon, but this time he knew he'd be back. His mother clung to him at the last, crying. Young Ana hung on too. "Don't forget me, Oscar. I want to go study." As he hugged his little sister, he assured her, "I won't forget you, Ana. I promise."

He told them goodbye at the door of their house, and his brother-in-law went along with them, helping to carry their bags to the center of the village. While there were no buses, the man was sure he could find a truck to give them a ride. Before rounding the corner, Salvador looked back. His family was still there, waving to him, and he saw that their handkerchiefs were at their eyes. His eyes too were dim with tears, but they were not bitter, sad tears this time.

Back in the city, at the ICC Receiving Center for babies and new children, Salvador was preparing to leave. He would be flying back to the university. But he still just had to call Mami Fleck! *She will be so happy for me!* he thought.

For the next hour, over international long distance, Salvador told me all about his visit to his village. There were times—especially when he told about making himself known to his mother—when he could no longer talk. He was weeping on one end of the line, and I was weeping on the other.

"Oh, Salvador! I am so happy for you? Do you remember a few days ago when we planned this trip? We had a special prayer that God would grant you the joy of finding whatever family there still was. Isn't God good! His love never fails."

"It is true, Mami. I want to tell you that I have never felt God's presence so real as the past few days. I can see, all through these years, even the worst of them, that God had His hand over us. I have been thinking that the God who delivered the children of Israel and took them through the Red Sea is the same God who made these past few days possible."

"You know," he told me, "just before I left, my mother asked me if I wouldn't come back and share what I've learned about the Bible and God with all of them."

My heart thrilled for him. "That is something I have been thinking about. I think you should plan to spend your summer vacation up in your village. You are going to be a minister. One of your first mission fields can be your family and your village."

At that, Salvador choked up again. "Nothing would

make me happier, Mami Fleck. I want to tell you that I can never find words to express my thanks to God, and to everyone who had a part in caring for me and loving me when I needed it so much. I'm especially happy that you introduced me to my wonderful Father in heaven."

"You know, Salvador, I've been like a mother to you, and you are a son to me. But I am happy beyond words that you now have your own real mother back again."

"Mami, remember one thing. You will always be a mother for me, and I love you just like I do my own mother."

"I know, Salvador. I believe that." I have to admit that I was really choked up at that point.

Then he added, "I was thinking about that day when the captain gave me his name. He had told me that I should be a soldier in their army, but then he said, 'My name is Salvador. I want to give you my name. I hope that someday you can save someone else.' Mami Fleck, I'm going to be a soldier, but not in that army. I will be a soldier in God's army and save souls for His kingdom."

Epilogue

*A*s this book goes to press, the story of the little rebel continues to unfold. Salvador is now in his senior year of theology and looking forward to the day when he will be a pastor. His letters are filled with stories of university life. As part of his training he has been named one of the elders of the university church and has preached from its pulpit. In his humble way he told me that one of his teachers talked to him afterward, saying, "It was one of the most inspiring sermons I have ever heard."

I don't know what he preached about, but he may have shared some of his story. He is still involved in musical activities as well as the outreach ministries of the Theology Department. When I asked him where he thought he might go when he graduates, he replied, "I don't know where the Lord will lead me, but I will go wherever that is."

During the Christmas break he went back to his village to visit his mother. I gave him some money for his fare and told him, "If you have some money left over, do something special for your mother."

Later he told me, "My mother didn't have indoor plumbing, and I was able to build her a septic tank and put in a toilet."

"How did you have enough money for that?" I asked him.

"I just purchased the cement and built it."

"You mean you built the whole thing! Does it work?"

He laughed. "Yes, I built the whole thing, installed water, and it works."

I knew that he'd learned a lot about building during his years at El Bosque. All the children learn to work, and the boys help lay blocks for the new houses and do inside plastering. But I never dreamed he would attempt to build a toilet!

"Mama was so happy with her new bathroom," he added.

Later Salvador sent me a beautiful handwoven tapestry that his mother made for me in appreciation.

I arranged for him to take his little sister, Ana, to El Bosque, so she could go to school. Professor Donaldo and his wife invited her to live at their house. It was hard for Magdalena to let her go, but Ana begged for the opportunity. Now Salvador had the position of elder brother and could be trusted to make that decision. Ken and I sponsor her, and she writes to us in Spanish, telling about her life in school. Juana tells me that Ana is learning quickly. She's in the fifth grade and adapting very well. We became acquainted when I visited El Bosque, so now I have another daughter who calls me "Mami Fleck."

Salvador plans to spend some time with his mother before starting out in his life's work. She doesn't read

Spanish, but she is eager for him to teach her about his faith. His dream is to hold evangelistic meetings in his village. Although Magdalena suffered so much and lived for years thinking her only son was dead, she doesn't begrudge the years they were apart. In her humble home in that isolated mountain village, she has the great joy of knowing that her son—her only son whom she thought she had lost forever—has come back. Her pride knows no bounds when she tells her friends, "My boy is studying to be a pastor."

Ruthie was thrilled to know that her birth parents are alive. Salvador sent her a letter from them, telling how happy they are to know that she is alive and well. They would love to see her, but are thankful that she has a Christian home with parents who love her. Ruthie has written to them, and hopes to eventually travel to their village to see the place where she was born and to meet the parents that she doesn't remember. She and her husband-to-be came to my office the other day to tell me of their plans to marry. They hope to visit her birth parents someday and put the final pieces of her life back in place.

As to Salvador's plans for marriage and a home of his own, that decision still remains to be made. He assures me that he is trusting God with that decision. For this coming vacation, between semesters, he plans to spend some time at El Bosque helping to build another house for children. Although he now has his childhood home back, he still thinks of El Bosque as his home. It was the place he found God, healing for his heart, and hope for his future.